JEAN'S
BEANS

Pictured on the front cover is
Chicken and Chick-Pea soup, olla Podrida, page 36.

ii

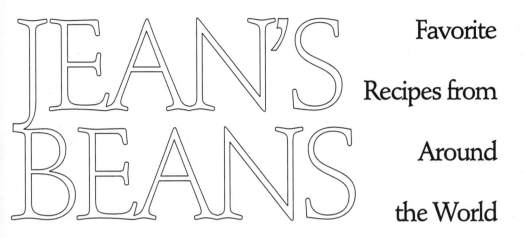

JEAN'S BEANS

Favorite Recipes from Around the World

JEAN HOARE

FIREFLY BOOKS

BOOKMAKERS PRESS

First Firefly Books Printing: 1995

Canadian Cataloguing in Publication Data

Hoare, Jean, 1914–
    Jean's beans : favorite recipes from around the world

Includes index.
ISBN 1-895565-67-7

1. Cookery (Beans).   I. Title.

TX803.B4H62   1995   641.6'565   C95-930890-3

A FIREFLY BOOK

Published by
Firefly Books
250 Sparks Avenue
Willowdale, Ontario
Canada M2H 2S4

Published in the U.S. by
Firefly Books (U.S.) Inc.
P.O. Box 1338, Ellicott Station
Buffalo, New York 14205

Photography by
Patricia Holdsworth Photography
Regina, Saskatchewan

Photo Design and Food Styling by
Margo Embury
Regina, Saskatchewan

Pottery Plates by
Don Chester and Jack Sures
Regina, Saskatchewan

Produced by
Bookmakers Press
12 Pine Street
Kingston, Ontario
K7K 1W1

Printed and bound in Canada by
Friesens
Altona, Manitoba

Printed on acid-free paper

Contents

Preface

Although the year was 1946 and the canvas-covered wagon that brought my wedding gifts and other effects from our first home in Ontario was moved by horsepower under a metal hood rather than by oxen, I still felt a close kinship with the true homesteaders who had preceded me west by a mere sixty years or so. Perhaps it was their example that kept me going during those first few years. In my imagination, I could picture the campfires and smell the smoke rising as the travelers rested in this beautiful valley that I still call home.

What did they bring with them from their former homes? How did they weather the difficult times? And what did they cook? For ten years I, too, was without modern "conveniences," and as I experienced the problems of storage of staples when temperatures could change in a matter of hours from 40 degrees below zero to 40 above, my respect for the likes of dried beans, peas, and lentils grew by leaps and bounds.

Later, as I followed up my interest in foods of the new and old worlds, I discovered that the world has been "full of beans" since way back. The Old Testament has many references to these dried seeds: Esau's selling of his birthright for a bowl of lentil soup in the Book of Genesis; stories of the nutritional goodness of beans in Daniel and Ezekiel. I have even found a report that before Pompeii was destroyed by the eruption of Mount Vesuvius A.D. 79, an enterprising business was sending sealed clay pots of chick-peas and bacon throughout the Roman Empire. A precursor of our present-day canned pork and beans!

Over the years, as I became more involved with food of all kinds, I started experimenting with my own version of baked beans. Never one to be content with basic recipes, I began combining as many varieties of beans as I could assemble. It might be just three or four, but often eight to ten different sizes, shapes, and colors would be mixed together. This mixture became known as Jean's Beans, of course!

Starting with my recipe for baked beans, I began a collection of recipes from all over the world, tracking down ideas that were typical of the country of origin or that caught my eye as being unusual and intriguing—perhaps the name, or some ingredient, or its use for special occasions. I began thinking of this search as my "bean stalk." As I tried out these recipes, sometimes minor substitutions had to be made, but the dishes were kept as true to the originals as possible. Here is my collection. Read, cook, and enjoy.

Nutrition Update

Beans — The Nutrition Dynamo

Beans, an international staple for thousands of years, are now one of the most sought-after gourmet ingredients. Designer food stores, as well as health food stores, from Toronto to Vancouver, from New York to San Francisco, report a dramatic increase in the demand for beans. Canadian Cancer Society guidelines, issued recently, suggest dietary measures to help reduce the risk of some cancers. Beans, with their high-fibre content, are right up there at the top of the list.

Nutrition studies conducted at the University of Toronto, by Dr. David J. A. Jenkins, have found that many people can lower their cholesterol, by 13-14%, by eating two servings of beans every day. Beans have three qualities that contribute to lower blood lipid (cholesterol) levels, insoluble fibre, their protein composition and starch. Beans, lentils, split peas, oats, barley, dense-grain breads and pastas, as "slow-release" carbohydrate foods, lower blood lipids and also help control diabetes by regulating blood sugar.

Except for soybeans, pulses (legumes) are low in fat. They are also low in sodium and are cholesterol-free. Beans, lentils and peas are high in fibre, iron, Vitamin-A and the B-Vitamins, thiamin, riboflavin and niacin, and vegetable protein. They contain good amounts of phosphorus and calcium and small amounts of other minerals. One cup (250 mL) of cooked navy beans contains 26% (15.8 g) of the daily iron needs, plus 63% of the folic acid requirements and about 13% of the calcium needed. Beans, in combination with grains, provide a good dietary amino acid (protein) balance. Try beans with rice (Bean Salad with Rice, page 102), pasta (Pistou with Pesto alla Genovese, page 33) and whole-grain breads (Boston Baked Beans with Brown Bread, page 54).

Beans provide low-cost nutrition and they have the added advantage of getting onto our plates without valuable nutrients being lost in refining or processing. They need no artificial preservatives or additives.

Over the years, with discoveries of new sources of food, the popularity of beans has fluctuated greatly. Beans have been called "poor man's food" because of their low price and ease of storing. But with our increased knowledge of what we should eat these Cinderella vegetables should assume their rightful place. I invite you to join me now and discover the wonderful world of bean cookery.

How It All Began

Baked beans built the West just as surely as that railway stretching from sea to sea. What would all those railway builders and settlers and explorers have eaten . . . if it hadn't been for beans?

Dried beans kept well, stored easily, and baked obligingly over the coals of a campfire or on the back of a kitchen range. They didn't ask much at the preparation stage but gave generously when it came time to eat. There were very few recipes, and homemakers and bachelors just did the best they could with what they had – a little bit of salt pork, an onion or two, sugar and molasses when they were available. The meals may not have been fancy, but cooking always tastes good when the world is young and working hard!

Speaking of working hard, the story is told of a young Mountie serving in a northern outpost who came up with a most innovative packaging idea for baked beans. It seems that he periodically baked a big batch of beans and then poured the finished product into long ladies' stockings. He hung the stockings on nails outside his cabin door and left them there to freeze solidly. Whenever he wanted a meal, he just chopped off a length of stocking and heated up the appropriate amount of beans. The first TV dinner? Perhaps, but I have to wonder how he kept himself in stockings!

A rancher from southern Alberta recalled that they used to pile baked beans on newspaper, freeze them, and then cut off pieces to take along on the trail. When chow time came, they'd throw the hunk of beans into the frying pan and have themselves a feast. However, he never cleared up for me the problem of the paper. Did they eat that too or did they fish it out of the pan when everything was bubbling? Was this a case of "all the news that's fit to eat"?

The modern version of this method recommends a heavy polyethylene sheet onto which the beans are poured and frozen. Once frozen, the sheet of beans is broken up and stored in clean bags. I expect to hear about this as a wonderful new idea for backpackers or mountain climbers or something. The more things change, the more they stay the same.

Cookbooks – including recipes for baked beans – started appearing in western Canada in the 1920s and 1930s, often written by women's groups trying to raise some money. These local cookbooks augmented the hitherto rather meagre supply of reference material. Some English housewives carried their copies of Mrs. Beeton's *Book of Household Management* with them; others had treasured handwritten collections of family favorites.

When, in 1928, the United Farm Women of Alberta published their cookbook, it would have been a welcome addition, a sign that homemaking was moving into a more sophisticated phase. Mind you, the recipes were still pretty matter-of-fact. From the UFWA cookbook, Ida Lundberg from the Sakawto local in Eckville gave this recipe for baked beans.

Recipe for Baked Beans

1	qt	beans
½	lb	sliced bacon
1	tsp	soda
1	tsp	mustard
1	tbsp	brown sugar
1	tsp	ginger
2	tbsp	molasses
1	tsp	salt

Soak beans overnight. In the morning, scald with hot soda water. Drain. Add fresh water and cook 15 minutes. Pour off all the water. Put beans in stone jar, add other ingredients. Cover with fresh water and bake for 4-5 hours with the cover on the jar. Remove cover for last half hour.

Bean soup was even more matter-of-fact. This recipe was signed by Mrs. A. B. Grieve from the Lougheed local UFWA.

Bean Soup

2	cups	beans
1		medium onion
3 or 4	cups	milk

Put beans to soak overnight in cold water. In the morning, put on to cook in fresh water to cover. Add the onion about an hour before they're done. Add milk and just bring to boiling point. Salt and pepper to taste.

Obviously you had to have some confidence and some common sense to tackle such barely explained recipes. However, that's how it used to be. Pioneers cooked as much from the seats of their pants as from the instructions in a book.

As far as beans are concerned, nothing much changed until the 1970s, when future shock hit us all. First of all, new Canadians began serving up their traditional and very tasty meals, many of which featured beans. We began to look at the lowly bean with more respect. Then nutritionists began talking about complete proteins and low-fat cooking and economical meals. Once again, the bean came up for air. Finally, farmers began experimenting with new bean crops and improving old bean crops. A pulse growers' association was organized in western Canada . . . and the bean was back.

The Basics of Beans

If You Knew Beans Like I Know Beans

Everybody knows something about beans, peas, and even lentils. But what about those other two words that crop up on the same subject — legumes and pulses? Quite simply, when they are growing in the field, beans, peas, and lentils are classified as annual legumes. The edible seeds removed from the pods are called pulses. Pulses can be used fresh, frozen, canned, or dried, and dried beans, peas, and lentils are what this book is all about.

It used to be sufficient to know a navy bean when you met one. That's about all we could buy. But no more! Canadian farmers are growing more and more varieties of beans, peas, and lentils, and we can buy more and more from other parts of the world. Here's a quick summary of some of the products now available.

Adzuki Beans (sometimes spelled Azuki) are very small, deep red beans that are extremely popular in Oriental dessert recipes. They are made into sweet sauces or pastes that can be used as a topping for sherbets or frozen on sticks like popsicles.

Black Beans are also called turtle beans. Black skinned with a creamy flesh, they are a staple of South American soups and stews. The Chinese ferment the cooked beans to produce a black bean sauce which is used in many of their recipes and which can be purchased in jars at Chinese specialty stores.

Black-eyed and **Yellow-eyed Peas** are also known as black-eyed beans and are sometimes confused with black beans. Although they are called peas, they are actually beans and have to be treated as such. Their names describe their appearance.

4

Garbanzo Beans are also known as chick-peas, ceci beans, and grams, just to keep everyone confused. They are light brown, round, and nutty tasting.

Lima Beans are generally green, sometimes white, mealy beans that come big or small. They are as important in some South American countries as the potato is in Ireland.

Kidney Beans are red-brown beans usually used in chili con carne. A white kidney bean is also beginning to show up in both dried and canned forms.

Mung Beans are the beans most often used for sprouting, and they are also used by the Chinese in desserts.

Pinto Beans are kissing cousins of the kidney bean. They are pink with brown freckles, which they lose during cooking.

Red Mexican Beans are small and oval. They retain their dark red color when cooked and may be substituted in recipes calling for red kidney beans.

Soybeans are the most nutritious of all beans and cause the least flatulence. They come in many colors. The average protein content of a bean is 20 percent; a soybean is 40 percent protein.

White Beans include navy beans, Great Northern beans, and pea beans. The Great Northern bean is the North American version of the French bean referred to as "haricot" or the Italian variety called "cannellini." These are all large white beans. A smaller French bean, comparing in size to the navy bean, is commonly called a "flageolet."

To Soak or Not to Soak

Beans must be soaked in water before they are used. Their skins are impermeable so water can only enter through the end formerly attached to the plant. This process of rehydration takes more or less time — depending on the type of bean — and can be done in two basic ways.

The Slow Soak

Wash beans. Remove any withered or broken beans and any bits of debris. For each cup of beans, use 3 cups of cold water. Cover beans with water and let soak for 8 to 12 hours or overnight. At the end of the soaking period, drain off the soaking water and proceed with recipe.

The Quick Soak

This is the preferred method for soaking beans as it is just as efficient as and less time consuming than the Slow Soak and there is no danger of the beans turning sour, something that can happen very easily.

Wash beans. Remove any withered or broken beans and any bits of debris. For each cup of beans, use 3 cups of cold water. Cover beans with water, bring slowly to a boil, and boil gently for 2 minutes. Remove from heat, cover, and let stand for 1 hour. Drain off soaking water and proceed with recipe.

Soaking Peas and Lentils

Beans must be soaked before cooking, but lentils (green or yellow, split or not) do not require presoaking. They can be cooked immediately, according to the recipe. Always wash lentils before using, and once washed, use right away because the process of rehydration begins as soon as water is added. Skim off any scum that forms as the lentils cook.

Peas like to be complicated. Split peas are more like lentils and therefore do not require presoaking before being used in recipes. However, black-eyed peas, yellow-eyed peas, and chick-peas are really beans and must be soaked before cooking. Use either the Quick Soak method above or the Slow Soak method on page 5, or check the instructions on the package. Things are moving so quickly in the bean field that new developments in growing and processing beans may change cooking methods.

Cooking Beans

Dried beans, peas, and lentils should be cooked slowly in water with some fat added. Use the following recipe when cooked beans are called for.

1	cup	dried beans	250 mL
3	cups	water (for soaking)	750 mL
2½	cups	water	625 mL
1	tbsp	vegetable oil	15 mL

Sort and rinse beans. Place beans in a heavy saucepan and cover with water for soaking. Bring to a boil. Boil for 2 minutes, remove from heat, cover, and let stand for 1 hour. Drain soaking water. Add fresh water and oil. Bring to a boil; reduce heat. Cover and simmer until beans are tender (1 to 3 hours depending on the type of bean). Makes 2 cups (500 mL).

In addition to stove-top cooking, beans can be baked in the oven or cooked in a pressure cooker or slow cooker. A pressure cooker is a great time saver. Combine soaked beans with water, vegetable oil, and seasonings and fill cooker no more than half full. Follow manufacturer's instructions for operation and begin timing once 15 pounds pressure has been reached. It is sometimes difficult to find the right setting for beans on a slow cooker. If the setting is too low, the beans may still be hard after 10 hours of cooking; if it is too high, the liquid will evaporate. Experiment with your own slow cooker and see how to get the best results. Microwave cooking is not recommended for cooking dried beans, peas, or lentils.

The following chart from *The Perfect Pulses . . .* cookbook by the Alberta Pulse Growers Association gives some guidelines for cooking times.

Soaked	In a Saucepan	In a Pressure Cooker*
Great Northern Beans	1–1½ hours	5–7 minutes
Navy Beans	1½–2 hours	6–8 minutes
Pinto Beans	1½–2 hours	7–9 minutes
Red Mexican Beans	1½–2 hours	7–9 minutes
Yellow or Green Whole Peas	1–1½ hours	5–7 minutes
Unsoaked		
Lentils	45 minutes	Not recommended

*After reaching 15 pounds pressure

A Note about Metric Conversions
Recipes in *Jean's Beans* are given in both standard and metric measurements. Most have been tested in standard measurements but have not been tested specifically with the metric measurements. The standard measurements have been converted to metric by a method known as common metric replacement, a method that does not produce exact equivalents but comes close. Exact conversions sometimes result in awkward fractions and sizes so the replacement method rounds up or down for ease in measuring.

Beans Must Be Boiled
Beans must be boiled for at least several minutes during the cooking process because they contain lectin, a toxin that can cause stomach cramps, nausea, and diarrhea if beans are not tender and cooked through before they are eaten. Since it's very hard to eat a bean that hasn't been thoroughly cooked, this warning is likely unnecessary. However, I include it just to be safe.

So It's Tough Beans, Is It?

If your beans refuse to get tender, even after proper soaking and cooking, there are a number of possibilities. For one thing, beans vary enormously from package to package depending on the variety of bean, the growing conditions for that particular crop, and the length of time the package has lingered on the shelves. Altitude makes a difference as well. The higher you are, the longer it takes to soak and cook a bean to tenderness.

Toughness can also be caused by hard water. Pioneer homemakers used to add baking soda to the soaking water to overcome the hardness of the water and make the beans tender faster. However, nutritionists frown on that practice nowadays because it can remove nutrients from the beans. It is better to cook them longer instead. In extreme cases of hard water, you can use purified drinking water for soaking and cooking beans.

Remember that acidic additions like tomatoes, vinegar, and lemon juice should not be added to a bean mixture until the beans are almost tender as the acid may retard the tenderizing process.

Cooking with beans is not an exact science, and sometimes you'll just have to conclude that you have a tough bean . . . one that needs the stuffing cooked out of it!

How to Puree a Bean

Wash beans, then soak by either Quick Soak method or Slow Soak method, pages 5 and 6. Cover with fresh cold water, bring to a boil for 10 minutes, reduce heat, and simmer until tender. Drain. Grind through a foodmill, or puree in a blender or food processor. You may have to add a bit of liquid saved from the cooking process, just enough to get the mixture moving. If you don't want bean skins in the puree, use a food mill, or force the puree through a fine meshed sieve.

Bean puree will keep for a day or so in the refrigerator, but it should be frozen if it's going to be kept any longer. One cup of dried Great Northern beans, soaked by either method, boiled 10 minutes, then simmered for 30 minutes, will yield 2⅔ cups (650 mL) puree. One cup of large lima beans prepared in the same way will yield 2 cups (500 mL) puree. If you are going to use the puree for dessert recipes, do not add any seasonings when you cook the beans.

Storing and Freezing

Dried beans, peas, and lentils will keep indefinitely in moisture-proof containers. Once the dried product is rehydrated and cooked it can be stored for one or two days in a refrigerator. For longer storage, it should be packaged in convenient serving sizes and frozen.

Beans freeze well. With one large bulk cooking, you can be ready for emergencies or for when you just feel like being lazy. Although microwaves are not recommended for cooking beans from a dried state, they do come in handy for thawing or reheating precooked bean dishes. In addition to freezing extra make-ahead meals, freeze containers of unseasoned bean puree to use in your favorite bean dessert recipes.

How Much Is Some?

It's difficult to be absolutely precise when discussing dried beans because 1 cup (250 mL) of dried navy beans will not produce exactly the same amount of cooked product as, say, 1 cup (250 mL) of dried garbanzo beans. Generally, dried beans will double and a bit more once they're soaked and cooked. Here are some general guidelines for the bean recipes that follow.

Dried Beans	Package Weight		Volume
Adzuki Beans	1 lb/450 g	=	2¼ cups/550 mL
Garbanzo Beans (Chick-Peas)	1 lb/450 g	=	2⅓ cups/575 mL
Great Northern Beans	1 lb/450 g	=	2⅔ cups/650 mL
Lentils	1 lb/450 g	=	2⅓ cups/575 mL
Lima Beans (large)	1 lb/450 g	=	2⅔ cups/650 mL
Mung Beans	10 oz/283 g	=	1½ cups/375 mL
Navy Beans	1 lb/450 g	=	2⅓ cups/575 mL
Pinto Beans	1 lb/450 g	=	2⅓ cups/575 mL
Red Kidney Beans	1 lb/450 g	=	2⅔ cups/650 mL
Split Peas	1 lb/450 g	=	2⅓ cups/575 mL

	Dried		Soaked
Great Northern Beans	1 cup/250 mL	=	2½ cups/625 mL
Large Limas	1 cup/250 mL	=	2–2¼ cups/ 500–550 mL

The Problem with Beans!

Some people do have a problem with digestion of the larger pulses, but something can be done about it. Research has shown that flatulence (the polite term for the gas caused by beans) is greatly reduced if the soaking water is discarded. The nutritional loss is minimal in comparison to the benefits. Don't waste the soaking water, though. It can be used to water your plants!

Start adding these terrific nutritional morsels to your regular diet, beginning with lentils, split peas, and mung beans, the three pulses least likely to cause any discomfort whatsoever.

It is also suggested that by starting with small servings, gradually increasing in volume and frequency, the body will produce the enzyme needed to eliminate this problem. In the many countries where pulses are a staple food, eaten daily in many cases, flatulence is unheard of.

Appetizers, Breakfast or Brunch Dishes, Anytime Snacking

While "stalking" for bean recipes, I kept turning up ideas for breakfast or brunch meals. In fact, I kept turning up recipes for any part of the day or night. We have taken beans for granted for so long that we're surprised once we realize how often we use them.

I love adventure. That's why I enjoyed the research on this book so much. Each of these recipes tells something about the area it comes from, something about those men and women who planted the crops, picked them, pounded them, cleaned and prepared them. Trying to recreate their recipes is like recreating a piece of their lives. The next best thing to being there, I always say.

The recipes included in this section come from many different parts of the world. Mexico, of course, is well represented, with recipes such as Bean Burritos and Mexican Bean Appetizer. Lebanon makes an appearance too with a chick-pea dip known as Hummus. Then there are hearty European breakfast dishes, and much more. Whatever the occasion, you will be sure to find a snacking dish that meets your needs.

Beans are versatile and they are delicious. There's always a way, I have learned, to work them into your diet. I invite you to join me on my "bean stalk" and sample some of the recipes presented in this section.

Bean Burritos

Some years ago, only those lucky enough to take winter holidays in Mexico were familiar with words like taco, nacho, tortilla, quesadillas, or burrito. Now we see them on our store shelves in many different forms. These thin, round cakes are made from flour or cornmeal and then wrapped, folded, stacked, or bent around various fillings. They are something akin to our hot dog or hamburger bun.

1		pkg. (12–15) small tortillas	1	
1		can (14 oz/398 mL) red kidney beans	1	
½	cup	minced red onion	125	mL
2	tbsp	chopped fresh cilantro or 1 tsp (5 mL) dried cilantro	25	mL
1	tbsp	freshly ground black pepper	15	mL
1	tbsp	chopped fresh oregano or 1 tsp (5 mL) dried oregano	15	mL

Notes: You can also use pinto or black beans. Cilantro, also known as Chinese parsley, is the lacy, fernlike top of coriander and it is sold fresh in stores that specialize in Oriental, Indian, or Latin foods. When sold fresh it should have the roots still on. Roots and tops should be wrapped in paper towels and kept in a plastic bag. (Do not use water as cilantro rots easily.) If necessary, it can be frozen. As for the freshly ground black pepper, that really does read 1 tbsp (15 mL). However, if that makes you nervous the first time, start with a quarter the quantity and taste and adjust for the future. Perhaps you will gradually work up to an asbestos tongue and go for a dash of hot red pepper sauce as well!

If tortillas were frozen, thaw them. If dried, soften them by frying quickly in lard, turning once, in a frying pan. If you're using corn tortillas and they are breaking as you roll them, try softening them a bit more by steaming them over hot water. Canned tortillas should be ready to use.

Drain beans, reserving about one-quarter of the liquid. Combine beans, reserved liquid, onion, cilantro, pepper, and oregano in a mixing bowl.

On each tortilla, spread 1½ tbsp (20 mL) of the bean mixture on one half of the circle. Roll once, tuck both ends toward the center, and continue rolling. Arrange in an oven-proof dish and cover with foil. Bake for 10 minutes in a 325°F (160°C) oven or until burritos are thoroughly heated. Serve at once. Makes 12 to 15 burritos.

Kitcherie

This mixture of rice and lentils or yellow split peas flavored with curry was commonly served in India for breakfast. British colonials preferred it without the lentils and added leftover bits of fish to the mixture instead, changing its name in the process to "kedgeree." This is the original version, still suitable for breakfast or brunch.

1		clove garlic, minced	1	
1		large onion, sliced	1	
⅓	cup	Clarified Butter (recipe follows)	75	mL
2	tsp	curry powder	10	mL
1	tsp	salt	5	mL
1	cup	dried lentils or yellow split peas	250	mL
2	cups	boiling water	500	mL
1	cup	uncooked rice	250	mL
		Boiling water, as needed		
2		hard-cooked eggs	2	

Note: This recipe is a good way to use up leftover cooked rice. Just put it into the mixture later in the cooking process and reduce the amount of water added.

In a large heavy saucepan, sauté garlic and onion in butter until onion is soft, about 10 minutes. Stir in curry powder and salt and sauté an additional 2 to 3 minutes. Add lentils or peas and stir until blended with butter and spices. Add boiling water, cover, and simmer about 15 minutes. Add rice and continue cooking until rice is tender. Add more boiling water, if necessary. When both lentils and rice are tender, uncover and place over low heat until water evaporates and mixture is dry. Garnish with quartered eggs. Serves 6.

Clarified Butter or Ghee

Heat butter very slowly until it melts. Remove from heat, allow milk solids to settle, and then skim off the clear butter fat for use in recipes that call for clarified butter or ghee.

Conquistadores named the hardiest strain of bean, the lima bean, after the place in which the Spaniards first tasted it . . . in Lima, Peru.

A Quiche for Real Men...
and Everybody Else Too!

Beans are very obliging. This recipe did not originally have beans in the ingredients but I put them there and they fit in wonderfully. The crust is whole wheat and the filling is vegetable and egg, which make this combination a healthy, wealthy, and wise way to eat!

Pastry

¾	cup	whole wheat flour	175	mL
½	cup	white flour	125	mL
½	tsp	salt	2	mL
½	cup	grated cheddar cheese	125	mL
½	cup	lard or shortening	125	mL
4–5	tbsp	cold water	60–75	mL

Filling

½	cup	sliced mushrooms	125	mL
½	cup	sliced celery	125	mL
½	cup	shredded carrot	125	mL
½	cup	chopped green pepper	125	mL
½	cup	chopped onion	125	mL
1		clove garlic, minced	1	
2	tbsp	vegetable oil	25	mL
1		can (14 oz/398 mL) kidney beans	1	
1	tbsp	brown sugar	15	mL
1	tsp	dried oregano	5	mL
1	tsp	chili powder	5	mL
1	tsp	dried sweet basil	5	mL
		Salt and pepper to taste		
4		eggs	4	
1	cup	milk	250	mL
2	tbsp	chopped fresh parsley	30	mL
1	cup	grated cheddar cheese	250	mL

Note: Canned green beans, drained, could be used in place of the kidney beans.

To make the crust, mix flours, salt, and cheese and cut in lard or shortening until the mixture resembles coarse crumbs. Add cold water, as needed, to make a smooth, fairly stiff dough. Grease a 10 inch (25 cm) quiche dish and line with pastry, leaving a good high rim. Prick pastry all over with a fork. To prevent the edges from falling down, line the crust with parchment paper (the kind of paper that lard comes wrapped in) and fill with dried beans. Another good use for dried beans! Bake for about 5 minutes in a 425°F (220°C) oven.

14

To make the filling, sauté mushrooms, celery, carrot, green pepper, onion, and garlic in oil until barely tender. If using canned kidney beans, drain and rinse several times before adding to vegetable mixture. Add sugar and seasonings and cook for another 5 minutes. Pour this mixture into the prebaked pie shell.

Beat eggs with milk, add parsley, and pour over vegetables in pie shell. Top with grated cheese. Bake for 25 to 30 minutes at 425°F (220°C) or until a knife inserted in the center comes out clean.

If desired, garnish with more vegetables in the last few minutes of baking. You could use rings of red or green pepper, slices of fresh tomato, or precooked stalks of asparagus arranged spoke-fashion on top. Makes one 10 inch (25 cm) quiche.

Guernsey Bean Jar

This recipe will give you great respect for the inventiveness and patience of cooks in an earlier time! I picked up this old recipe and story written by Mrs. Louise Helmot from a local newspaper when I visited the Channel Islands recently.

"Until the 1920s, Guernsey Bean Jar was the usual Guernsey breakfast. A few still so indulge. Some recipes give cow heel in place of pig's trotter and also include salt and pepper. Indeed, of some thirty recipes for this gastronomic delight that this editor has collected, no two are identical."

1	lb	dried haricot beans	500	g
1		pig's trotter or beef shinbone, or both	1	
1	lb	onions	500	g
1	lb	carrots	500	g
		Thyme, sage, parsley (to taste but use plenty)		

Note: Great Northern beans are ideal in recipes that call for haricots.

Soak beans overnight. Place ingredients in an earthenware jar and cover with water. Bring to a boil and then simmer for 8 hours, adding more water when necessary.

When this dish was eaten for breakfast, the method would be reversed with the presoaking taking place during the previous day and the long slow simmering left to the night hours, perhaps in the oven or on the back of a wood-burning stove. Those of us who are not lucky enough to have a wood-burning stove will have to make do with a low gas or electric oven set at 250°F (125°C). Makes 6 to 8 servings.

Jugged Haricots

The French version of the Guernsey Bean Jar is called Jugged Haricots. *Haricots* because that is the French word for beans and *jugged* because the mixture is stewed in an earthenware bean pot – a jug, in other words! The French add wine, otherwise the recipe is very similar.

1	lb	dried haricot beans	500 g
		Red wine to cover	
1		pair pig's trotters or pork hocks	1
1	lb	onions	500 g
		Salt and pepper to taste	

Wash and pick over beans. Place in an earthenware bean pot and cover with red wine. Add meat, onions cut in thick slices, and salt and pepper to taste. Stew very slowly, all day or all night, on the back of a woodstove or in a slow oven. Makes 6 to 8 servings.

Mary Salloum's Hummus Bi Tahini

This is a quick, easy, and delicious dip that we're starting to enjoy more frequently in Canada. Keep canned chick-peas and sesame seeds on hand and you'll always have the makings. Serve with small pieces of pita bread or crackers or crisp leaves of romaine lettuce. I'm indebted to Mary Salloum, the author of *A Taste of Lebanon,* for this recipe.

1		can (19 oz/540 mL) garbanzo beans	1	
¼	cup	Tahini Paste (recipe follows)	50	mL
1–2		cloves garlic, peeled	1–2	
½	tsp	salt	2	mL
¼	cup	lemon juice	50	mL
		Parsley sprigs		
		Lemon wedges		

Note: You can buy Tahini Paste at most supermarkets, or you can make your own using the recipe that follows. If you make your own, you can put all the ingredients for the hummus into the blender at once.

Drain beans and reserve liquid. Put beans into a blender or food processor. Add Tahini Paste, garlic, salt, and lemon juice. Blend for several minutes until completely smooth. Add some of the reserved bean liquid to make the mixture about the consistency of thick mayonnaise. It should mound when placed in a bowl or on individual serving plates. Garnish with parsley sprigs and lemon wedges. Mary Salloum always makes a small indentation in the top of the mound and sprinkles in a small amount of olive oil. Makes 2 to 2½ cups (500 to 625 mL).

Hot Mexican Bean Dip with Tostados, page 17

Tahini Paste

¼	cup	sesame seeds	50 mL
2	tbsp	water	25 mL
1	tbsp	vegetable oil	15 mL

Roast sesame seeds by placing in a pie plate in a low oven, about 250°F (125°C). Shake the plate periodically and watch very carefully. You want the seeds browned, not blackened. When finished, place in blender with water and oil. Blend until smooth. Makes about ¼ cup (50 mL).

Hot Mexican Bean Dip with Tostados

Tostados are small cocktail-sized tortillas that can be purchased fresh, frozen, or canned. After thawing (if using the frozen variety), cut into small chip-sized pieces and fry in shallow oil—or in lard as they do in Mexico—about 2 minutes a side. Drain on paper towels and serve with the following fiery dip.

½	lb	ground beef	250 g
¼	cup	chopped onion	50 mL
¼	cup	extra-hot ketchup	50 mL
1½	tsp	chili powder	7 mL
½	tsp	salt	2 mL
1		can (14 oz/398 mL) red kidney beans	1
½	cup	grated cheddar cheese	125 mL
¼	cup	green or black olives	50 mL
¼	cup	chopped raw onion	50 mL
		Tostados and/or corn chips for dipping	

Notes: If you can't get extra-hot ketchup, increase the chili powder. Increase it anyway if you like your chili hot. The chopped raw onion used for garnish at the end may be prepared from large cooking onions or green onions using both white and green parts for color interest.

In a heavy frying pan, brown ground beef and ¼ cup (50 mL) chopped onion. Remove any excess fat, then add ketchup, chili powder, and salt. Leaving the liquid on the beans, puree in a blender or mash very thoroughly by hand. Add to the meat mixture and heat through to blend flavors.

When ready to serve, spoon meat and bean mixture into a container that will keep the mixture hot. An electric frying pan, electric wok, or chafing dish over a heat source will all work fine. Garnish the top of the mixture with a circle of grated cheese around the outer edge, a circle of stuffed olives, and finally, in the center, the chopped raw onion. As the guests dip in their tostados or corn chips, the garnishes work down into the mixture, which is exactly what is supposed to happen! Have more garnishes on hand to add as needed. Makes approximately 4 cups (500 mL).

This is an ideal snack for such occasions as watching the Grey Cup or the Rose Bowl Parade on television. It stays warm and can be topped up without the host or hostess missing a single play or float! Also, it can easily be doubled or tripled to fit the crowd and the length of the party.

Pesto, Cheese and Beans

This molded appetizer, with its layers of red, white and green, is made in advance. Chilling overnight firms up the mixture for ease in unmolding at serving time. Alberta-grown Red Mexican beans give the best colour, but other red or spotted beans may be substituted.

Red Bean Layer —

2	cups	cooked beans (1 cup/250 mL dry beans)	500	mL
¼	cup	minced cooking onion	50	mL
2	tbsp	bacon or ham drippings	30	mL
¼	tsp	Tabasco sauce	1	mL
1		package (1¼ oz./35 g) taco seasoning mix	1	

Pesto Layer —

1	cup	snipped fresh basil, firmly packed	250	mL
¾	cup	grated Parmesan and/or Romano cheese	175	mL
½	cup	snipped parsley, firmly packed	125	mL
¼	cup	pine nuts, walnuts or almonds	50	mL
2		garlic cloves, quartered	2	
⅓	cup	olive oil or cooking oil	75	mL

Cheese Layer —

8	oz.	cream cheese	250	g
4	oz.	Camembert or Brie cheese	125	g
½	cup	heavy (whipping) cream	125	mL

If using canned beans, drain and rinse, then drain very well. Mash or purée cooked beans. Soften onion in bacon or ham drippings, but don't brown. Add to bean purée; add taco seasoning mix. Add Tabasco sauce, and mix well. Taste and adjust seasonings. Set aside until other mixtures are prepared.

In heavy-duty blender or food processor, blend all pesto ingredients until smooth. Remove rind from Camembert or Brie. Bring cheeses to room temperature. In medium-sized bowl, whip cream cheese and Camembert or Brie together until smooth. In a small bowl, beat cream until soft peaks form. By hand, fold whipped cream into the cheese mixture.

Assembly — Line a tall 6-cup (1.5 L) mold with a double layer of plastic wrap, fitting it down inside, to cling to shape of mold. Leave edges several inches above top. If desired, a double layer of cheesecloth can be used which will give the traditional markings of Coeur a la Creme. The first layer to put into the mold will be the top when it is turned out for serving. If mold tapers considerably adjust the quantities so the layers are approximately the same thickness. Spread ¼ of the cheese mixture in container, making sure it goes out to the edges. Top with ¼ of the pesto. Repeat these two layers, then add layer of beans, about ½ cup (125 mL), smoothing each layer out to the edges. Repeat with the ¼ of cheese mixture, ¼ of pesto, and another ½ cup (125 mL) of beans. The final layers consist of balance of cheese, then pesto, and remaining beans, about 1 cup (250 mL), which will be the base of the turned-out mold. Fold over the plastic wrap (and cheesecloth, if using) and press lightly over all 11 layers. Chill thoroughly.

Before serving, carefully lift back plastic wrap from the top and centre serving platter over mold. Turn over and remove mold. Carefully remove plastic wrap and cheesecloth. If desired, sprinkle top lightly with paprika, and garnish with sprigs of fresh basil. Serve with firm crackers or thin slices of baquettes. Corn chips or small pieces of tortillas can also be used. Offer small spreaders or butter knives. Yield — 5½ to 6 cups (1.5 L) total for 11 layers.

Note: If desired, layers may be cut down to 5, arranging them in a more shallow container. However, the effect will not be as dramatic.

Mexican Bean Appetizer

Make this in a clear, straight-sided dish, if possible, because the layers are so attractive—so is the taste!

1		can (16 oz/454 g) refried beans	1	
1	cup	sour cream	250	mL
2		ripe avocados, cubed	2	
1	cup	sliced black olives	250	mL
1		can (4 oz/114 mL) green chilies, chopped	1	
½	cup	chopped onion	125	mL
3		tomatoes, finely chopped	3	
1	cup	grated cheddar cheese	250	mL
		Nacho chips, corn chips, crackers		

Layer ingredients in the order given. Serve with a large bowl of chips for dipping. Makes about 4 cups (1 L).

Bean Rabbit

Do you say "rarebit" or "rabbit"? I vote for "rabbit," but no matter what the name, this cheese topping for toast makes a good late-night snack or a tasty light meal at any time of the day. With this version, you can also use up the last of the baked beans!

2	cups	cold baked beans	500	mL
¼	cup	butter	50	mL
½	tsp	paprika	2	mL
½	tsp	salt	2	mL
½–1	cup	milk	125–250	mL
1½	cups	grated sharp cheddar cheese	375	mL
		Pieces of toast or split and toasted English muffins		

Note: You can use canned pork and beans instead of leftover baked beans—one 14 oz (398 mL) can.

In a bowl, mash beans with a fork. Prepare chafing dish if you intend to serve the rabbit at the table. Otherwise, get out your double boiler. Melt butter in top part of pan over direct heat. Stir in paprika, salt, and mashed beans. As the mixture heats, stir in ½ cup (125 mL) milk. Slowly add cheese. The remaining milk can be added if the mixture is still too thick. At this point, take off direct heat and put over boiling water. Continue to cook, stirring occasionally, until cheese is completely melted and mixture is piping hot.

Serve over plain toast or toasted English muffins. Serves 4 to 6.

Ceci Snacks

These delicious nibblers are made from the beans that have four names: chick-pea in most English-speaking countries and in France, gram in India, garbanzo in Spain, Mexico, and the Philippines, and ceci in Italy. I chose the Italian name. You can start from dried beans, soaking and cooking them until they have just a touch of crunch left. If you use canned beans, you'll have a softer product, but still good if eaten at once.

1	lb	dried garbanzo beans	500	g
½	cup	butter	125	mL
2		cloves garlic, minced	2	
½	tsp	dry mustard	2	mL
1	tsp	chili powder	5	mL
2	tsp	salt	10	mL
1	tsp	ground ginger	5	mL
1	tbsp	soy sauce	15	mL

Note: You can use 2 cans (19 oz/540 mL each) garbanzos in place of the dried beans.

Prepare dried beans according to one of the methods outlined on pages 5 and 6. Cover drained beans with fresh water, bring to a boil for 10 minutes, then simmer about 30 minutes or until almost tender. You want some crunch left. Drain thoroughly.

In a heavy frying pan, melt half the butter. Add garlic and half of the partially cooked garbanzos. Stir over low heat until the beans are golden brown outside and tender inside. In a bowl large enough to hold what's in the frying pan, mix together mustard, chili powder, and salt. Add the hot, garlicky beans and toss well.

Put the other half of the butter into the frying pan and add remaining beans, browning as above. In another large bowl, mix ginger and soy sauce. Pour in second half of bean mixture and toss until beans are well coated.

Serve these two nibblers hot with cocktails or add to clear soups instead of croutons. Makes about 4 cups (1 L).

These snacks can be made ahead of time and frozen. To reheat, spread them on a cookie sheet while still frozen and place in a hot oven (400°F/200°C) for about 5 minutes. Always refrigerate or freeze any leftovers.

Soups

The great old writer Anonymous has said that "the discovery of a new dish does more for the happiness of man than the discovery of a new star." Now, that might be a bit strong, but food remains one of our greatest pleasures. And when the food is satisfying to the soul as well as satisfying to the body, then we've got a winner.

Which brings us to the matter of soups, one of the best foods for keeping body and soul together. In fact, soup has long been looked upon as a cure-all. A French proverb says that a well-made soup keeps a coin from the doctor's pocket, which is another way of saying what our mothers used to say—that a bowl of chicken soup will fix us right up.

So, I've included in this chapter the classics that use beans, peas, or lentils: Minestrone, Split Pea Soup, Black Bean Soup. And then, for fun, I've included some new and different soups that use beans: Nine-Bean Soup, Gypsy Soup, Bean Soup in a Buttercup. Try some. You'll wonder why you've neglected soups all these years!

Nine-Bean Soup

I have a kindred spirit who lives near Houston, Texas. Loretta Symm came up with a wonderful idea for soup . . . and for gifts! She makes up a big batch of mixed dried beans, lentils, peas, and pearl barley. Then she packages the mixture into smaller amounts to use at home or to give away (with recipe enclosed) as quick and tasty gifts. You might call this the soup version of my signature recipe, Jean's Beans. If you can't get exactly the mixture suggested below, just get as many as you can.

The Soup Mix requires 1 lb (500 g) each of

> **Dried yellow split peas**
> **Dried green split peas**
> **Dried black-eyed peas**
> **Dried black beans (turtle)**
> **Dried red beans (kidney)**
> **Dried pinto beans**
> **Dried navy beans**
> **Dried Great Northern beans**
> **Dried red lentils**
> **Barley pearls**

Mix up thoroughly, then divide into 2 cup (500 mL) portions and package in small plastic bags.

Now to make the soup, you will need

2	cups	Soup Mix	500	mL
8	cups	water	2	L
1	lb	ham, diced	500	g
1		large onion, chopped	1	
1		clove garlic, minced	1	
½	tsp	salt	2	mL
1		can (19 oz/540 mL) tomatoes	1	
1		can (4 oz/114 mL) green chilies	1	

Prepare dried beans according to one of the soak methods outlined on pages 5 and 6. Cover soaked and drained beans with water. Boil, covered, for 10 minutes, reduce heat, and simmer for 30 to 45 minutes or until beans (especially the navy beans) are beginning to get tender. Add ham, onion, garlic, and salt and continue simmering for another 45 minutes, or until beans are tender. Don't drain the tomatoes, just chop them up with the green chilies and add to the soup mixture. Simmer for another 30 minutes, stirring occasionally. Makes 8 cups (2 L) soup.

Minestrone alla Genovese

Minestrone, one of the best known vegetable soups, is never complete without a full complement of beans! Sometimes it also contains rice or macaroni, which changes the character of the soup somewhat – not to mention the name. But always it should be garnished with herbs, including basil. Here's one version – Minestrone alla Genovese.

½	cup	dried white beans	125	mL
4	tbsp	butter	60	mL
1	cup	fresh or frozen peas	250	mL
1	cup	diced zucchini	250	mL
1	cup	peeled and diced carrots	250	mL
1	cup	peeled and diced potatoes	250	mL
⅓	cup	sliced celery	75	mL
2	oz	salt pork, cubed (optional)	75	g
2	tbsp	chopped onions	25	mL
½	cup	chopped leeks	125	mL
2	cups	canned tomatoes	500	mL
8	cups	chicken stock	2	L
1		bay leaf	1	
2		sprigs fresh parsley	2	
1	tsp	salt	5	mL
		Freshly ground black pepper to taste		
½	cup	uncooked white rice	125	mL
		Pesto (see page 34) or Herb Garnish (recipe follows)		
		Parmesan cheese		

Note: You need about 1 lb (500 g) unshelled peas to produce 1 cup (250 mL) peas.

Prepare dried beans according to one of the soak methods outlined on pages 5 and 6. Once drained of the first water, cover again with water, bring to a boil for 10 minutes, reduce heat, and simmer for 1 to 1½ hours or until just barely tender. Drain thoroughly and set aside.

In heavy frying pan, melt butter over moderate heat. Add peas, zucchini, carrots, potatoes, and celery. Tossing constantly, cook 2 to 3 minutes until lightly coated with butter but not browned. Set aside.

If using salt pork, render cubes in the soup pot until crisp and brown. Remove pieces with a slotted spoon and set aside to drain. (For vegetarian method, use 1 tbsp/15 mL cooking oil in place of the fat from the salt pork.) Stir onions and leeks into fat or oil, stirring constantly for about 5 minutes until vegetables are soft and lightly browned. Drain tomatoes; chop and stir in with vegetables from the frying pan, chicken stock, bay leaf, parsley, and salt and pepper. Bring back to a boil and then simmer, partially covered, for 25 minutes. Remove bay leaf and parsley. Add rice, cooked beans, and salt pork (if using) and cook for final 15 to 20 minutes or until rice is tender. Taste and adjust seasonings.

Serve with Pesto or Herb Garnish and Parmesan cheese.

Herb Garnish

1	tbsp	finely chopped fresh basil or 1 tsp (5 mL) dried basil, crumbled	15	mL
1	tbsp	finely chopped fresh parsley	15	mL
½	tsp	finely chopped garlic	2	mL

Mix and sprinkle over bowls of soup.

Cream of Split Pea Soup

Split peas, green or yellow, have been used in soups all over the world—not just in Canada's province of Quebec! Madame Jehane Benoit, Canada's first lady of the kitchen, uses the green split pea in her soup on the basis that it is larger and tastier than its yellow split pea cousin. In most cases, split peas do not have to be soaked before cooking but Madame Benoit does, so since this is her original recipe, I have kept the soaking instructions.

1½	cups	dried green split peas	375	mL
6	cups	hot water	1.5	L
1		meaty ham bone	1	
1		onion, chopped	1	
½	cup	diced celery	125	mL
2	cups	milk	500	mL
1	tbsp	butter	15	mL
1	tsp	chopped fresh mint	5	mL
		Salt and pepper to taste		
		Croutons		

Note: If you don't have fresh mint, you can use the dried variety—about ½ tsp (2 mL).

Rinse split peas and soak overnight in enough cold water to cover. Next day, drain and place peas in a large saucepan and add hot water, ham bone, onion, and celery. Cover and simmer over low heat for 2 hours, stirring occasionally.

Remove ham bone; press peas through a food mill or puree in a blender or food processor. Put the puree back into the saucepan and add milk, butter, mint, and salt and pepper to taste. Simmer for a few minutes and serve with buttered croutons. Serves 6.

Bean Soup in a Buttercup

You bake and serve this soup in any one of the winter squashes: Hubbard, acorn, butternut, pumpkin, or my favorite, the buttercup. Prepare the pumpkin or squash by cutting off enough of the top to make a lid and then cleaning out the membranes inside. Drain upside down while the beans are simmering.

1		large winter squash or pumpkin	1	
2	cups	dried white beans	500	mL
8	cups	water	2	L
4		slices bacon, diced	4	
1	cup	chopped onion	250	mL
½	cup	chopped celery	125	mL
1		clove garlic, minced	1	
		Salt and pepper to taste		
½	tsp	dried sweet basil	2	mL
¼	tsp	dried oregano	1	mL
		Heavy cream (optional)		
		Shelled pumpkin or sunflower seeds, toasted		

Prepare dried beans by either of the soak methods outlined on pages 5 and 6. To soaked and drained beans, add water, bring to a boil for 10 minutes, then simmer about 20 minutes or until beans are about half cooked.

Meanwhile, in a frying pan, fry bacon until crisp. Remove and drain on paper towel. In bacon fat remaining, sauté onion, celery, and garlic until onion is tender but not brown. Add sautéed vegetables to beans, stir in seasonings, and continue simmering soup until beans are very soft, about 1 hour.

While the soup cooks for this last hour, put the prepared squash or pumpkin in a deep casserole or heavy Dutch oven. Tuck lid beside the squash, not on top. Bake in a 350°F (180°C) oven until the meaty flesh begins to soften. The cooking time will vary depending on the kind and size of squash used. If liquid collects in the bottom of the shell, spoon it out and discard. When a fork will pierce the meat (do this gently—you don't want to puncture the shell), fill the shell with the bean mixture, leaving about a 1 inch (2 cm) space below the lid. Cover squash with its own lid and return to medium oven (350°F/180°C) for about 20 minutes more or until the squash is very tender but still retains its shape.

For a thicker soup, remove one or two cups of the bean soup, mash or puree it, and return to the shell, stirring it in carefully. If a richer soup is desired, add heavy cream until the consistency suits your taste. Return to oven for reheating about 10 minutes before serving.

Take whole squash or pumpkin to the table (in the dish in which it has been baking—don't try to move it) and impress your guests all to pieces by serving the soup from the shell, spooning out a bit of the squash or pumpkin flesh along with the soup. Sprinkle each serving with toasted seeds. Serves 6 to 8.

For a quick and easy version of this recipe, use canned soups. Try a combination of split pea and ham mixed with bean and bacon. Dilute them with water, milk, or heavy cream to suit your taste. The number of cans needed will vary with the size of the pumpkin or squash chosen. Add the canned soup to the precooked squash, leaving a 1 inch (2 cm) space below the lid. Cover squash with its own lid and return to medium oven (350°F/180°C) until soup is piping hot and squash is very tender but still retains its shape. Test often as you don't want to overcook the shell and have it collapse, like London Bridge!

Ev's Soup, Back from Disaster

After two days of fussing to make the perfect consommé for a dinner party, my friend Ev spilt the whole kit and caboodle on the kitchen floor. Luckily, she had a well-stocked emergency shelf from which she plucked a can of split pea soup with ham and went on to make a delicious soup that tasted like it had been simmering for days—just as good as the poor old consommé! For simpler occasions, try combining two or more of the excellent canned soups so readily available nowadays and invent your own "super soup."

1		can (10 oz/284 mL) split pea soup	1	
1		can (10 oz/284 mL) condensed tomato soup	1	
1		can (10 oz/284 mL) condensed mushroom soup	1	
1	cup	milk	250	mL
1		can (4 oz/113 g) shrimp	1	
1		can (4 oz/120 g) flaked crabmeat	1	
¼	tsp	curry powder	1	mL
½	cup	dry sherry	125	mL
		Chopped fresh parsley		

In a large saucepan, mix soups and heat thoroughly. Add milk. Drain, rinse, and redrain shrimp. Drain crabmeat. Add both to soup. Add curry powder. Just before serving, add sherry. Sprinkle each bowlful with chopped parsley. Serves 8.

Black Bean Soup

Black beans have an interesting flavor and texture and are especially good in soup. Try them this way for your first time!

1	lb	dried black beans	500	g
½	cup	vegetable oil	125	mL
1½	cups	chopped onion	375	mL
4		cloves garlic, minced	4	
1		meaty ham bone or smoked ham hock	1	
12	cups	water	3	L
1	tbsp	ground cumin	15	mL
2	tsp	dried oregano	10	mL
1		bay leaf	1	
1½	tsp	salt	7	mL
1	tsp	pepper	5	mL
		Pinch of cayenne pepper		
3	tbsp	chopped fresh parsley	50	mL
½		sweet red pepper, diced	½	
¼	cup	dry sherry	50	mL
2	tsp	brown sugar	10	mL
2	tsp	lemon juice	10	mL
		Sour cream or Crème Fraîche (recipe follows)		

Prepare dried beans according to one of the soak methods outlined on pages 5 and 6.

Heat oil in a large soup pot or Dutch oven. Add onions and garlic and cook over low heat until onions are soft and transparent. Place meat into the pot; add water and drained beans. Stir in half the cumin and all the oregano, bay leaf, salt, pepper, cayenne pepper, and parsley. Bring to a boil, reduce heat, and simmer, uncovered, until beans are tender and liquid has been reduced to about one-quarter its original amount (about 2 hours).

Remove bones and cut meat into small pieces. Return to the soup. Add the rest of the cumin, sweet red pepper, sherry, brown sugar, and lemon juice. Simmer another 30 minutes, stirring frequently. Correct the seasonings and serve very hot, garnished with either sour cream or Crème Fraîche. Serves 4 to 6.

Crème Fraîche

Crème fraîche, a French specialty, is a naturally matured, slightly sour-flavored raw cream. Although it is available at some gourmet shops, it's easy to make at home. Use in salad dressings or as a topping for fruits and berries.

| 2 cups | heavy whipping cream | 500 mL |
| 2 tbsp | commercial buttermilk | 25 mL |

Mix cream and buttermilk and allow to sit at room temperature for 6 to 8 hours. The texture will be similar to commercial sour cream. Cover and refrigerate at least 24 hours before using. Keeps refrigerated for several weeks. Makes approximately 2 cups (500 mL).

Potage Paul

At a gathering of people interested in good food and good wine, I met Beverly Sutherland Smith of Australia. Beverly is the author of *A Taste for All Seasons*, a beautiful cookbook that includes the following recipe for a creamy dried green pea soup. She calls for Surprise peas, and to my surprise, I was able to find them in Canada. "Surprise" is the trade name for quick-dried dehydrated garden peas, but if you're not able to find your "surprise," use any good-quality dried green peas.

¼ cup	butter	50 mL
1	onion, chopped	1
1	clove garlic, minced	1
3	large lettuce leaves, chopped	3
2 tbsp	chopped fresh parsley	30 mL
½ tsp	curry powder	2 mL
4 cups	chicken stock	1 L
2 tbsp	Surprise peas (see above)	30 mL
2 tsp	cornstarch	10 mL
1 tbsp	water	15 mL
½ cup	cream	125 mL
	Salt and pepper to taste	

Note: You can use either half-and-half or whipping cream.

Melt butter in a heavy saucepan or Dutch oven. Sauté onion, garlic, lettuce, and parsley until soft. Add curry powder and fry a moment. Add stock and peas. Cook, covered, for 30 minutes. Puree mixture in a food mill or blender and return to pot. Mix cornstarch with water, add to the soup, and stir until thickened. Lastly, add cream and adjust for seasonings. Makes 6 servings.

The old Mexican word for bean is ayacotl, *which has been corrupted to* haricots, *the generic term used in France for all beans.*

Garbure with Goudale

This old French classic is a main-course, hearty peasant soup full of vegetables – especially beans and cabbage. The final mixture is thick enough for the ladle to stand up in the center of the tureen. It is served in two courses. First the meat and vegetables are spooned over savory-coated slices of bread. Then to the broth left in the tureen, a cup of red or white wine is added, making it a goudale, which the diner drinks. It is the goudale that inspired the French proverb "A well-made goudale keeps a coin from the doctor's pocket."

14	cups	water	3.5	L
1½	lb	meat	750	g
2	cups	peeled and diced potatoes	500	mL
1	cup	peeled and diced carrots	250	mL
1	cup	peeled and diced turnips	250	mL
¼	cup	chopped leek, white part only	50	mL
2	lb	cabbage, cut into long thin shreds	1	kg
6		whole cloves	6	
2		onions	2	
2		cloves garlic, minced	2	
		Bouquet garni (see below)		
2	cups	cooked beans	500	mL
		Salt and pepper to taste		
		Toast, garlic toast, or garlic croutons		
1	cup	red or white wine	250	mL

Notes: For the meat, you may use smoked ham, salt pork, boneless game, or preserved goose. You may use canned or home-cooked navy or fava beans. You may also want to use fresh beans – broad, fava, or scarlet runner in season.

To make the bouquet garni for this recipe, put into a cheesecloth or tea infuser the following: 6 sprigs parsley, 1 bay leaf, ½ tsp (2 mL) each thyme and marjoram.

In a large heavy soup pot or Dutch oven, bring water to a boil. Add meat in a whole piece. Add potatoes, carrots, turnips, leek, and cabbage. Put 3 cloves into each onion; add to the soup. Stir in garlic. Add bouquet garni and return everything to a boil. Partially cover the pot and simmer for 2½ hours or until meat is tender. Add cooked beans in the last 15 minutes. Once meat is cooked, remove and discard the bouquet garni and season broth with salt and pepper to taste. Remove meat and cut into serving-sized pieces to serve along with the soup. Garbure may be held at this point and reheated just before serving.

To serve, place a piece of toast – plain or spread with garlic butter – or garlic-flavored croutons in the bottom of an individual deep soup dish.

Using a slotted spoon, serve the vegetables over the toast and pass the sliced meat. To the broth left in the soup pot, add wine. Serve this part of the soup in cups or small soup bowls with handles so that it can be drunk along with the garbure. Serves 8 to 10.

Gypsy Soup, olla Gitana

The Gypsies (or Romanies as they prefer to be called) are members of a wandering race with Hindu origins, mistaken by many as coming from Egypt. This unusual, intriguing soup is fruity, a little bit nutty, and altogether terrific.

1	cup	cooked chick-peas	250	mL
1	cup	cooked white beans	250	mL
9	cups	water	2.25	L
½	tsp	salt	2	mL
1	cup	fresh green beans	250	mL
1	cup	cooked pumpkin	250	mL
3		small pears, peeled and diced	3	
1	tbsp	vegetable oil	15	mL
1		clove garlic, crushed	1	
1		slice white bread	1	
1		medium onion, chopped	1	
2		tomatoes, peeled and chopped	2	
1	tsp	paprika	5	mL
		Few strands of saffron or powdered saffron (optional)		
10		almonds, ground	10	
2	tbsp	vinegar	25	mL
		Pepper to taste		

Notes: See pages 6–7 for information on preparing cooked beans. Cooked squash or sweet potato could be used in place of pumpkin.

Place water in a large soup pot along with salt, chick-peas, white beans, green beans, pumpkin, and pears. Cover and simmer for 20 minutes until green beans and pears are tender.

Meanwhile, heat oil in a frying pan; add garlic and bread. Fry over medium heat until bread is browned on both sides. Remove bread from frying pan and set aside. Using same oil, fry onion until soft and transparent, adding more oil if necessary. Add tomatoes and paprika and cook 5 minutes longer. Remove frying pan from heat.

At this point, you make a puree—either by hand or in the blender—of saffron, garlicky bread, and ground almonds. Add tomato mixture from the frying pan plus vinegar. Add pepper to taste. Stir puree into the soup. Cover and simmer for 10 minutes, just enough to heat through. Serves 6.

Esau's Pottage

According to the Old Testament, Esau sold his birthright for a "mess of pottage." He must have loved lentil soup! There are many versions of his favorite pottage (see below for some suggestions), but try this one first and see if you agree with Esau.

1		meaty ham bone or smoked ham butt	1
6	cups	water	1.5 L
1½	cups	dried lentils	375 mL
1		large onion, chopped	1
2		stalks celery, with leaves, chopped	2
1		large carrot, sliced	1
		Salt and pepper to taste	
		Bouquet garni (see below)	

Note: To make bouquet garni, in cheesecloth or tea infuser, place pinch of thyme, 3 whole cloves, 4 peppercorns, 3 sprigs parsley, 1 bay leaf, and 1 clove garlic.

Simmer ham bone in water for 1 hour. Wash and pick over lentils. Add to meat along with onion, celery, carrot, salt and pepper, and bouquet garni. Bring to a boil, reduce heat, and simmer, partially covered, for about 1½ hours or until the lentils are thoroughly cooked. Remove meat and bouquet garni.

Puree the soup in a blender—in small batches, if necessary. Return to the pot, heat through, and season to taste. Dice ham butt or meat from ham bone and add back into the soup or serve separately.

Serve in soup plates, sprinkled with a bit of chopped parsley. Enough for 6.

For a lighter soup, remove vegetables and seasonings after cooking is completed. Serve the resulting clear broth with cubed ham and/or sliced cooked frankfurter.

For a richer, creamier soup, add scalded light cream just before serving, being careful not to boil the soup after the cream has been added.

Middle Eastern versions use lamb and lamb stock in place of the ham, often adding tomatoes or tomato puree and putting mint in the bouquet garni instead of the thyme and bay leaf.

If you don't want to puree the lentil and vegetable mixture, sautéing the vegetables in butter before adding them to the soup enhances their flavor.

In an emergency, use a canned ham instead of the ham bone or butt and dice or slice to serve with the broth.

Pistou with Pesto alla Genovese

What did we do before we had food processors and blenders? We used mortars, pestles, and a lot of elbow grease, that's what. The food was placed into the round mortar and then pounded into a paste with the pestle. One such paste, the pesto paste, got its name from having been made this way. Pesto is a fresh basil sauce that can be served over pasta, tucked into cherry tomatoes for a colorful appetizer, or used as a garnish for soups, as in the following recipe.

First, the pistou, the soup mixture.

¼	cup	olive oil	50	mL
1		large onion, diced	1	
3		fresh tomatoes—peeled, seeded, and chopped	3	
6	cups	water	1.5	L
		Salt and pepper to taste		
¾	cup	partly cooked white beans	175	mL
½	lb	fresh green beans	250	g
2		medium zucchini, diced	2	
3		medium potatoes, peeled and diced	3	
2		leeks (bulbs and greens), chopped	2	
2		stalks celery (with leaves), chopped	2	
2	tbsp	minced fresh parsley	25	mL
¼	lb	vermicelli, broken up	125	g
		Pesto (recipe follows)		

Notes: You may use about 1 cup (250 mL) canned tomatoes in place of the fresh tomatoes. Instead of fresh green beans, you could use one package (10 oz/284 mL) frozen, straight-cut green beans. As for the white beans, white kidney or Great Northern would be best, and the cooked beans should still be firm.

Heat olive oil in a large soup pot and sauté onion until transparent. Add tomatoes and simmer, uncovered, until the tomatoes are soft, about 10 minutes. Stir frequently. (Canned tomatoes would not require this cooking time.) Add water, seasoning, white beans, vegetables, and parsley. Bring to a boil; reduce heat and simmer for 20 minutes.

Meanwhile, parboil vermicelli in salted water, about 5 minutes on a full boil. Drain and add to the soup. Continue cooking for another 10 minutes, or until everything is cooked.

Stir approximately 1 tbsp (15 mL) of Pesto into each soup bowl when serving. Grated Parmesan, Romano, or Gruyère cheese may also be offered. Serves 6 generously.

Pesto alla Genovese

2	cups	coarsely chopped fresh basil leaves	500	mL
1	tsp	salt	5	mL
½	tsp	freshly ground pepper	2	mL
1–2	tsp	minced garlic	5–10	mL
2	tbsp	chopped pine nuts	25	mL
1–1½	cups	olive oil	250–375	mL
½	cup	Grated Romano and/or Parmesan cheese	125	mL

Notes: If fresh basil leaves are not available, the best substitute is fresh flat-leafed Italian parsley with 2 tbsp (25 mL) dried basil leaves added. Whichever herb you use, strip the leaves from the stems and discard the stems. Then coarsely chop the leaves and pack tightly to measure. Adjust the proportion of Romano cheese (strong and sharp) to Parmesan (milder) to suit your own taste.

If you're a determined purist, you can make this by hand with a mortar and pestle. If not, fire up the blender or food processor. Combine basil, salt, pepper, garlic, and pine nuts with 1 cup (250 mL) olive oil. Blend or process at high speed, stopping the machine every few seconds to push herbs down with a spatula. Continue until ingredients are smooth and sauce is thin enough to run off the spatula. Add up to ½ cup (125 mL) more olive oil if the mixture seems too thick. Scrape out into a bowl and stir in the grated cheeses. To store, run a film of olive oil over the top, cover, and keep in the refrigerator. Makes 1½ to 2 cups (375 to 500 mL).

An old turn-of-the-century cookbook advised that beans should be cooked "until the skins burst—best determined by taking a few beans on the tip of the spoon and blowing on them." The beans thus blown upon must be thrown away, the instructions revealed. The water that was used for boiling the beans was also to be thrown away—out of doors, not in the sink. Just why the sink couldn't take the bean water, I'm not sure, but it may have had something to do with whether or not the sink had a drain connected to it!

United States Senate Bean Soup

This is as close as I can come to the genuine Senate bean soup. It's the addition of mashed potatoes to the beans that makes it distinctive. The soup was the creation of Henry Cabot Lodge Sr., and a Congressional resolution requires that it be served every day in the Senate dining room.

½	cup	dried navy beans	125	mL
1		ham bone	1	
4	cups	boiling water	1	L
½		bay leaf	½	
3–4		peppercorns	3–4	
3		whole cloves	3	
1		carrot, diced	1	
3		stalks celery, with leaves, diced	3	
½		onion, chopped	½	
1		clove garlic, minced	1	
⅛	tsp	saffron	0.5	mL
½	cup	mashed potatoes	125	mL
½	cup	chopped fresh sorrel	125	mL
		Croutons and chopped chives		

Notes: You can also use Great Northern, white kidney, or large lima beans. You can substitute chopped fresh spinach or romaine lettuce leaves for the sorrel. Add 1 tsp (5 mL) lemon juice to the spinach or lettuce to approximate the sorrel tang. If you haven't got a ham bone, substitute 2 oz (75 g) salt pork.

Prepare dried beans by either of the methods outlined on pages 5 and 6. Put drained beans into the soup pot, cover with boiling water, return to boil for 10 minutes, then simmer until soft, about 1½ to 2 hours. Alternatively, you could begin with 1 cup (250 mL) cooked or canned white beans, in which case, you'd skip all of the above and simply put beans into a pot with about 2 cups (500 mL) of boiling water.

To the tender beans, add ham bone or salt pork, bay leaf, peppercorns, and cloves. Simmer another hour. Add carrot, celery, onion, garlic, saffron, mashed potatoes, and sorrel. Simmer another 30 minutes. Remove ham bone or salt pork. Take any ham off bone and cut into small chunks. If using salt pork, remove it and cut into small chunks. Set aside.

Place soup into a food processor, blender, or food mill. Blend or sieve until smooth. Thin with boiling water or hot milk if it seems too thick. Taste and adjust seasonings. Serve with cut-up meat, croutons, and chives. Makes 4 cups (1 L).

Chicken and Chick-Pea Soup, olla Podrida

Best known of all Spanish foods is the paella, a thick stew of seafood (whatever was caught that day), some meat, some fowl, tomatoes, onions, peppers, and garlic—all of which is thickened with saffron-seasoned rice. The following soup using chick-peas (also known as garbanzo beans) is much simpler to make but tastes a lot like paella. I like to add to the illusion by topping each serving with a few mussels. The result is so beautiful that I hate to tell you that the literal translation of the Spanish name of this soup is "rotten pot."

1	cup	dried chick-peas	250	mL
1		2–2½ lb (1 kg) frying chicken	1	
4	cups	water	1	L
1		can (14 oz/398 mL) chicken bouillon	1	
1		can (14 oz/398 mL) tomatoes	1	
¼	cup	tomato paste	50	mL
1		clove garlic, minced	1	
½	cup	chopped onion	125	mL
⅓	cup	chopped green pepper	75	mL
2	tbsp	vegetable oil	25	mL
1		can (4 oz/114 mL) green chilies, diced	1	
1	tsp	salt	5	mL
		Pinch of saffron		
12		mussels in shell (optional)	12	
1	cup	garlic croutons	250	mL

Note: You may also use canned chick-peas. About 2 cups (500 mL) canned should be the equivalent of 1 cup (250 mL) dried. Drain them well before using.

If using dried chick-peas, prepare them according to one of the soak methods outlined on pages 5 and 6. In a heavy 4 quart (4 L) soup pot, combine soaked and well-drained chick-peas, chicken, water, and bouillon. Boil for 10 minutes, reduce heat, cover, and simmer until chicken is tender (about 30 to 40 minutes). Remove chicken. When cool enough to handle, remove meat from bones, discard bones, dice meat, and set aside.

If using dried chick-peas, continue to simmer peas and stock another 30 to 40 minutes or until chick-peas are tender. If using canned chick-peas, add to chicken stock without further cooking. Add tomatoes, tomato paste, and reserved chicken pieces. Stir well.

In a small frying pan, sauté garlic, onion, and green pepper in oil until onion is tender but not brown. Add this mixture to the soup pot. Stir in chilies, salt, and saffron. Bring everything to a boil, reduce heat, and simmer for 15 minutes.

If using mussels, wash well in running water, scrubbing shells with a stiff brush. Clip off beards with scissors, if necessary. Lay the tightly closed shells on top of the soup mixture for the last 6 to 8 minutes of cooking, or until shells open. Discard any mussels that open before they're cooked or that fail to open after cooking.

To serve, ladle into soup bowls, top with mussels (if used), and sprinkle with croutons. Serves 4 to 6.

Salads

Beans of all sorts have moved into the spotlight in restaurant salad bars. What would a salad bar be without three-bean salads, four-bean salads, bean sprouts, and chick-pea garnishes?

The great advantage of using beans in a salad is that they are readily available all year round, not just in certain seasons. Drained canned beans can quickly be made into a salad by the simple addition of a tasty marinade. And there's no end to the combinations that can be made. Use canned beans only or canned beans plus fresh vegetables such as broccoli, cauliflower, and green or wax beans.

Be sure to blanch the fresh vegetables used with beans in a salad. About 2 minutes is enough for fresh green beans; broccoli and cauliflower need about 5 minutes; carrot sticks need 8 to 10 minutes, depending on their size. Be sure not to overcook any of the fresh vegetables. They should still be crunchy crisp and a bright color. Frozen vegetables do not require the blanching. Just thaw them and use.

Bean and fresh vegetable salads can be kept for several days in the refrigerator – another great advantage. In fact, they're best made at least a day ahead so the flavors have a chance to mix and blend.

Anyway, I begin this chapter with the salad version of Jean's Beans . . . a salad that uses as many different kinds of beans as possible. And then I go on to other new, different, and delicious salads that star beans.

Jean's Beans in a Jar

Don't be restricted to three-bean or five-bean salad combinations. Get out your best clear glass bowl and start building a rainbow. Or, if you plan on taking bean salad to a picnic, build it in a glass jar or Pyrex container with a screw top, choosing the size suitable for the number of people involved. Make sure you've got a tight-fitting lid, and you're away to the races.

Use one or more of the following varieties of bean

> **Dried beans that have been soaked according to either of the methods outlined on pages 5 and 6 and cooked until tender**
> **Canned beans that have been rinsed, if necessary, and drained well**
> **Fresh or frozen beans, cooked just long enough to be tender but still crisp**

Other vegetables you can add

> **Thinly sliced white or red onions**
> **Rings of sweet red or green pepper**
> **Niblet corn**
> **Diced celery**

Layer the beans and other vegetables in your bowl or jar so that colors and textures alternate. Then pour over a clear oil and vinegar dressing and allow the salad to marinate for at least several hours. Allow approximately ½ cup (125 mL) per person. Extras or leftovers can be stored in the refrigerator for up to four days.

Cabbage, Apple, and Bean Slaw

When your regular coleslaw recipes begin to lose their appeal, try adding cooked lima beans. Not only are you perking up an old favorite, but you're adding nutrition as well.

1–2	cups	cooked lima beans	250–500 mL
3	cups	shredded cabbage	750 mL
1–2		red apples, cored and diced	1–2
½	cup	cubed cheese	125 mL
¾	cup	Blender Mayonnaise (recipe follows)	175 mL

Notes: Homemade mayonnaise is definitely best for this recipe. As for the cheese, Swiss with its big holes is nice; so is Gruyère.

Mix all the ingredients with the mayonnaise. Enjoy. Serves 6.

Blender Mayonnaise

1		egg	1	
1	tsp	dry mustard	5	mL
½	tsp	salt	2	mL
		Dash cayenne pepper		
1	tsp	sugar	5	mL
¼	cup	salad oil	50	mL
½	cup	salad oil	125	mL
3	tbsp	fresh lemon juice	50	mL
½	cup	salad oil	125	mL

Note: This mayonnaise is easily made in a blender. It is even easier with one of the new hand-held stick blenders.

In the blender or mixing bowl, put egg, dry mustard, salt, cayenne pepper, sugar, and ¼ cup (50 mL) oil. Blend or beat until completely combined. With motor going, pour the next ½ cup (125 mL) oil slowly into the blender along with the lemon juice. When that begins to thicken, add remaining ½ cup (125 mL) oil and blend a few seconds longer until thick. Taste and adjust seasonings. Makes about 1½ cups (375 mL).

Black-eyed Pea Salad

This simple salad makes an attractive addition to a buffet table.

1	cup	dried black-eyed peas	250	mL
2	tbsp	salad oil	25	mL
3	tbsp	wine vinegar	50	mL
½	cup	chopped onion	125	mL
½	cup	chopped fresh parsley	125	mL
1		clove garlic, minced	1	
1	tsp	dried basil	5	mL
½	tsp	dried oregano	2	mL
¼	tsp	dry mustard	1	mL
		Healthy dash of freshly ground pepper		
		Red pepper flakes to taste . . . carefully!		
		Green pepper rings or lettuce leaves		

Rinse and cook black-eyed peas in plenty of water until they're tender but not mushy. Drain. Combine all the remaining ingredients in a bowl and pour over the warm drained peas. Toss gently. Cover and let marinate overnight. To serve, line a shallow bowl with green pepper rings or lettuce leaves. Heap the peas in the center. Makes 6 servings.

Rainbow Layered Bean Salad

This recipe has specific instructions, just in case you don't want options when you're preparing salad for supper!

1		can (19 oz/540 mL) green beans	1	
		Celery, cut diagonally into thin slices		
1		can (19 oz/540 mL) garbanzo beans	1	
2	cups	cooked black beans	500	mL
		Red onion, sliced thinly into rings		
1		can (19 oz/540 mL) lima beans	1	
1		can (19 oz/540 mL) kidney beans	1	
		Blender Vinaigrette (recipe follows)		

Note: Black beans are not always available in canned form, but they look very nice in a layered salad so I included them in this combination. If you just don't have the time or the inclination to prepare the black beans from scratch, substitute another canned bean, one with some variety in color or texture.

Drain all the beans, saving the juice for soups or stews. Rinse beans if they're gooey—particularly kidney beans. Drain again.

Layer the ingredients in the order they've been listed and pour Blender Vinaigrette or your own favorite clear oil and vinegar dressing over the layers. If you don't want to layer the salad, simply mix the beans and other vegetables together and toss with the dressing. Serve on lettuce or arranged in an attractive bowl to 10 people.

Blender Vinaigrette

This is a basic herb vinaigrette and can be used on various fresh vegetable salads.

1	cup	salad oil	250	mL
⅓	cup	vinegar	75	mL
2	tbsp	fresh lemon juice	25	mL
1		clove garlic, crushed	1	
1	tsp	salt	5	mL
½	tsp	freshly ground pepper	2	mL
4	tbsp	chopped fresh dill	60	mL
½	tsp	dried basil	2	mL
4		sprigs Italian flat-leafed parsley	4	

Note: You can use 2 tsp (10 mL) dry dill weed if you don't have fresh dill.

Put everything into a blender or food processor and buzz until garlic is completely blended into the dressing. Store in a jar in the refrigerator and shake before using. Makes 1½ cups (375 mL).

South Seas Salad

For more than a quarter of a century, The Flying N restaurant was known for serving a fresh fruit salad in a hollowed-out pineapple shell. The Hawaiian-style baked beans in this book (Here Today, Gone to Maui, page 82) can also be served in a pineapple shell. So to keep up my reputation with pineapple boats, I present Beans in Boats, otherwise known as South Seas Salad.

1		fresh pineapple	1
1		fresh papaya	1
1		can (10 oz/284 mL) mandarin orange sections	1
1½	cups	fresh bean sprouts	375 mL
1	cup	cooked garbanzo beans	250 mL
⅓	cup	canned water chestnuts, sliced (optional)	75 mL
1		green onion, finely chopped	1
1	cup	cooked diced meat	125 mL
		Papaya Seed Dressing or Macadamia Cream Dressing (recipes follow)	

Notes: If fresh pineapple is not available, use canned pineapple, drained well. Save the juice. If fresh papaya is not available, you can use fresh apple tossed in the juice from the pineapple to prevent darkening. You may use cooked chicken, turkey, or roast pork for the meat portion of this recipe.

To prepare the pineapple boats that make this salad really special, cut fresh pineapple in half lengthwise, starting at the base and ending by cutting through the leaves. Cut each half into half again if the pineapple is very large. Ideally, you would use smaller pineapples and serve one half to each guest. Cut out the hard center core and remove the flesh from the shell. Dice enough of the pineapple to measure 1 cup (250 mL). Drain well, reserving juice. Keep the remaining fruit for some other purpose.

Cut papaya in half, scooping out the small black seeds and setting them aside for Papaya Seed Dressing—if that's the dressing you have selected. Peel, then dice papaya, sprinkling it lightly with pineapple juice to keep it from darkening. Drain mandarin orange sections. Wash and drain bean sprouts. Rinse and drain garbanzos and water chestnuts, if using.

In a large enough bowl, combine fruit, beans, water chestnuts, green onion, and meat. Toss lightly with one of the dresssings on page 43. Serves 4 as a main course; 6 to 8 if part of a buffet.

Papaya Seed Dressing

This dressing is excellent with either fruit salads or tossed green salads.

1	cup	sugar	250	mL
1	tsp	salt	5	mL
1	tsp	dry mustard	5	mL
1	cup	tarragon vinegar	250	mL
1	cup	salad oil	250	mL
1		small onion, diced	1	
3	tbsp	fresh papaya seeds	50	mL

Note: Plain white vinegar may be used in place of the tarragon vinegar.

Place sugar, salt, dry mustard, and vinegar in a blender. Start motor and gradually add salad oil and onion. When thoroughly blended, add the papaya seeds. Blend only until the seeds are the size of coarsely ground pepper. Makes about 3 cups (750 mL).

Macadamia Cream Dressing

⅓	cup	sour cream	75	mL
3	tbsp	Blender Mayonnaise (see page 40)	50	mL
1	tbsp	orange-flavored liqueur	15	mL
½	cup	macadamia nuts	125	mL

Notes: Orange-flavored liqueurs include Cointreau, Grand Marnier, and Orange Curaçao. Almonds or pistachios can be substituted for the macadamia nuts.

In a small bowl, stir together sour cream, mayonnaise, and orange liqueur. Chop nuts coarsely and fold into sour cream mixture. Spoon on top of fruit salad or pass separately. Makes about 1 cup (250 mL).

Greek Chick-Pea Salad

The Greeks are well acquainted with the pleasures of goat's-milk cheese, as are cooks all over Europe, who have known and used feta cheese for centuries. The feta cheese used here turns up in almost every "Greek" salad . . . and for good reason! Try it. It's a spirited, quick, easy, and delicious way to enjoy the flavor of another country.

Dressing

1	tsp	Dijon mustard	5	mL
½	tsp	salt	2	mL
⅝	cup	salad oil	150	mL
¼	cup	fresh lemon juice	50	mL
		Healthy dash of freshly ground pepper		

Salad

1		can (19 oz/540 mL) garbanzo beans	1	
½		red onion	½	
2	oz	feta cheese	60	g
1	tbsp	chopped fresh parsley	15	mL
		Lettuce leaves		

Make the dressing first by combining the first five ingredients in a blender and mixing thoroughly. Or you could shake the dressing ingredients in a glass jar with a tight-fitting lid until completely blended.

Drain garbanzos (also known as chick-peas) well. Cut onion into thin slices and separate into rings. Mix beans and onion together. Pour dressing over and toss well. Marinate for at least an hour.

At this point, you could keep the salad in the refrigerator for several hours or several days. When ready to serve, crumble feta, add parsley, and toss with the bean mixture. Serve on lettuce leaves. Serves 4 to 5.

Sousboontjies, A Bean Pickle

While on my "bean stalk," some unexpected help came from my friend Mrs. Lesley Faull whose Silwood House in South Africa is the equivalent of Cordon Bleu cooking schools in France. She sent along a calendar that combined postcards of scenes from South Africa with recipes. One of the recipes involved—wouldn't you know it—beans! She calls for sugar beans, which obviously aren't the sugar-snap beans we eat—pods and all, so I experimented a bit and came up with lima beans as a good substitute.

1	cup	cooked small lima beans	250	mL
2	tbsp	butter	25	mL
2	tbsp	sugar	25	mL
¼	cup	vinegar	50	mL
		Salt and pepper to taste		
		Cornstarch and water, if needed		

If using dried lima beans, soak according to one of the methods outlined on pages 5 and 6. Cover drained beans with fresh water and cook until tender. If using canned beans, rinse and drain.

Add to the beans, butter, sugar, vinegar, and seasonings to taste. Place on top of stove and simmer on lowest heat for 15 minutes. Thicken with cornstarch, if needed, about 1 to 2 tsp (5 to 10 mL) cornstarch dissolved in 1 tbsp (15 mL) water. Serve either hot or cold as an accompaniment to meat. Makes 1 to 1½ cups (250 to 375 mL).

Green Bean and Chick-Pea Salad

This recipe offers double value—fresh green beans and canned chick-peas (garbanzos), both complemented by a basil-flavored dressing.

1	lb	fresh green beans	500	g
1		can (19 oz/540 mL) garbanzo beans	1	
¼	cup	chopped green onion (with tops)	50	mL

Dressing

2	tbsp	white wine vinegar	25	mL
1	tbsp	chopped fresh basil	15	mL
		Salt and pepper to taste		
1		large clove garlic	1	
4	tbsp	salad oil	60	mL

Note: If you don't have fresh basil, you can use 1 tsp (5 mL) dried basil.

Top and tail green beans and cut crosswise in 2 inch (5 cm) pieces. Steam until just barely tender, about 6 minutes. Drain and rinse garbanzos. Mix green beans, garbanzos, and onions together.

In a small bowl or screw-top jar, combine remaining ingredients and whisk or shake to mix. Let dressing stand for 15 minutes to allow flavors to blend. Remove garlic clove and add the dressing to the bean mixture, tossing well to coat. Chill for at least an hour before serving to 6 to 8 guests.

Spinach and Pinto Salad

There's such good taste and nutrition in this salad that it deserves a more beautiful name—something like Salads Make My Day . . .

1		head lettuce	1	
½	lb	fresh tender spinach	250	g
2	cups	cooked pinto beans	500	mL
1		mild onion	1	
½		long English cucumber	½	
3		stalks celery	3	
		Spicy Tomato Dressing (recipe follows)		

Note: You may use iceberg, Boston, or green-leaf lettuce.

Wash and trim lettuce and spinach. Tear into bite-sized pieces and put into a salad bowl. Drain beans and rinse, if necessary. Slice onion, cucumber, and celery. Add all four to the salad bowl. Pour Spicy Tomato Dressing over the salad, toss gently, and serve immediately. Serves 6 as a main course or 8 if it is to accompany other food.

Spicy Tomato Dressing

⅓	cup	tomato juice	75	mL
1	tbsp	salad oil	15	mL
1	tbsp	fresh lemon juice	15	mL
1		clove garlic, crushed	1	
½	tsp	paprika	2	mL

Blend the dressing ingredients together or combine in a jar with a secure lid and shake vigorously. Makes about ½ cup (125 mL).

Mexican Taco Salad

I have taken my famous Mexican Bean Dip (page 17) across Canada with me because it's so handy to serve at book signings and demonstrations. Here's the salad version with an accompanying Green Chili Salsa, a snappy chili dressing that goes well with various bean dishes.

1½	cups	Green Chili Salsa (recipe follows)	375	mL
4	tbsp	salad oil	60	mL
1	tsp	cumin or chili powder	5	mL
6	cups	shredded lettuce	1.5	L
2	cups	canned kidney beans	500	mL
1		avocado, cubed	1	
2	tbsp	fresh lemon juice	25	mL
2		fresh tomatoes, peeled and diced	2	
½	cup	sliced ripe olives	125	mL
1	cup	shredded cheese	250	mL
		Taco chips for nibbling with the salad		

Prepare Green Chili Salsa. In a small jar, combine 1½ cups (375 mL) chili dressing with oil and cumin or chili powder. (You can add more or less spice to taste.) Mix well, or shake well if you're using a screw-top jar. Set aside until salad is constructed. Freeze remaining dressing for another time.

In a large salad bowl, preferably glass, place lettuce across the bottom and up the sides. Rinse and drain beans and arrange over lettuce. Toss avocado with lemon juice to keep it from darkening. Arrange over beans. Finish off with tomatoes and olives.

Just before serving, shake the dressing again and pour over the salad, tossing lightly. Pass shredded cheese – cheddar, longhorn, or Monterey Jack – and tacos. Serves 10 to 12 generously.

Green Chili Salsa

Ready-made bottled sauces are available, but even the ones marked "mild" may have more fire than you expect. By making your own you are in control – and it's less expensive.

1		can (14 oz/398 mL) tomatoes	1
1		can (4 oz/114 mL) chopped green chilies	1
2		green onions, chopped	2
1		clove garlic, minced	1
2	tsp	chili powder	10 mL
¼	tsp	each ground cumin, dried oregano, and salt	1 mL

Mix all ingredients together in a medium-sized saucepan. Cover and simmer for 10 minutes. Serve warm or chilled. Makes about 2 cups (500 mL).

Loire Valley Salad

On a recent trip with the International Wine and Food Society, I was introduced to a number of varieties of French goat's-milk cheese or *chèvre* cheese. The creamy styles were served in little rolls on cheese and fruit trays; drier and firmer varieties were used in salads; and the firmest varieties of all were breaded and then fried.

½	lb	Ribier grapes (dark blue)	250 g
½	lb	small, tender zucchini	250 g
2	cups	fresh bean sprouts	500 mL
4	oz	chèvre cheese	125 g
2	tbsp	salad oil	25 mL
1	tbsp	white wine vinegar	15 mL
1	tsp	sugar	5 mL
		Salt and pepper to taste	

Note: If you can't find fresh chèvre cheese, feta is probably the best texture for this salad. If you find it too salty, soak it in milk until it suits your taste. Gruyère or brick cheese could also be used.

Cut grapes in half and remove seeds. Slice or dice zucchini. Sort over bean sprouts, washing and draining well, if necessary. Cube or crumble chèvre, depending on the texture. Mix all four ingredients together. In a small bowl, combine oil, vinegar, sugar, and seasonings. Toss with the first mixture.

Nice accompaniments to this salad are thick slices of French bread, sliced tomatoes, and olives. Serves 5 as a side salad or 4 for a main luncheon dish.

Red Bean and Plum Sauce

This is a spicy, tasty accompaniment for meat and vegetable dishes—something like a chutney or relish. Slovakian countries are known for fruit growing, and this recipe calls for red kidney beans with damson plum jam. The result is terrific.

1		can (14 oz/398 mL) red kidney beans or 2 cups (500 mL) cooked red kidney beans		
1		small clove garlic	1	
		Pinch of salt		
½	tsp	crushed dried red pepper	2	mL
½	tsp	dried basil	2	mL
1	tsp	ground coriander	5	mL
½	cup	plum jam	125	mL
2	tbsp	red wine vinegar	25	mL
		Lettuce		

If beans are canned, drain and rinse lightly under cold running water. If beans start from dried state, follow soaking instructions on page 5 or 6 and then cover with fresh water and cook until tender, about 45 minutes, testing after 30 minutes as beans should not be overcooked.

Put garlic, salt, red pepper, and spices into blender. Buzz until mixed. Add jam, thinning as you go with vinegar, added slowly. If jam is runny, reduce amount of vinegar added to 1 tbsp (15 mL).

Fold sauce into beans. Let stand at room temperature for 2 to 3 hours or in the refrigerator overnight. Warm up again to room temperature before serving in a lettuce-lined bowl with cold meats and rolls. Makes 2½ cups (625 mL).

White Bean Salad

This is a most attractive salad with the white beans, orange sections, and bits of green. It's tasty also! It's taken from *The Perfect Pulses . . .* cookbook put out by the Pulse Growers Association of Alberta.

1	cup	dried white beans	250	mL
½	cup	chopped green onion	125	mL
¼	cup	diced green pepper	50	mL
2	tbsp	chopped fresh parsley	30	mL
1		large orange, peeled and diced	1	
1	cup	diced cooked salami sausage (optional)	250	mL

Dressing

¼	cup	salad oil	50	mL
2	tbsp	fresh lemon juice	25	mL
1		clove garlic, minced	1	
½	tsp	salt	2	mL
¼	tsp	pepper	1	mL

Note: Substituting diced red pepper for the green makes a very Christmassy-looking combination.

Prepare beans by one of the methods outlined on pages 5 and 6. Drain and cook in fresh water until tender, about 1 to 1½ hours. Drain again and let cool. Add vegetables, parsley, orange, and sausage (if used) to cooled bean mixture.

Mix oil, lemon juice, garlic, and seasonings together. Pour over beans and vegetables and toss gently. Serve at room temperature. Serves 6.

This combination is a good choice for a buffet since it's colorful and different from the usual assortment of salads.

Traditional Baked Beans and Chili

When it comes to cooking beans, we have come a long way from those basic bean recipes noted down by pioneers to the Canadian West. Traditional baked bean recipes, however, remain favorites, and in this section I have included old and new variations on those good old baked bean recipes that bring back happy memories of good food and good friends. And what better way to start the section than with the recipe that evolved along with my interest in beans, Jean's Beans.

I have also included a number of variations on another old favorite, chili. You may have thought chili was a straightforward matter of combining kidney beans, ground meat, tomatoes, and seasoning in a pot and cooking the mixture until it is thick and tempting. Not so. Chili is the source of much controversy. There are some people who swear up and down that chili must never include beans, only meat and seasonings. There are others who say beans are okay . . . if they're served alongside the meat, not mixed in with it. There are others who say they want beans in their chili, never mind what the so-called experts say. So I have included four different recipes for chili. The first one doesn't include beans in the mixture. The next one is chili with beans, but with some other wonderful differences. And the other two recipes are more traditional — crowd pleasers for both cook and consumers.

Jean's Beans, The Recipe That Started It All

My beans are seldom the same twice in a row, which has made it very hard to come up with a specific recipe! What makes Jean's Beans different from traditional baked beans is the variety of beans I use. Along with the navy beans generally used, I add Great Northern, pinto, large and small lima, pink, kidney, and red Mexican beans; black-eyed and yellow-eyed peas or chick-peas (garbanzos); or as many of these varieties as I have on hand when I get the urge to bake beans. Also, I use a whole onion, studded with cloves, which adds a wonderful flavor to the whole pot but is easily avoided by those who find onion hard to digest. (Sometimes the blame for discomfort suffered after eating baked beans should be directed to other ingredients in the pot, such as onions and molasses.) Finally, Jean's Beans are happy to be as flexible as you choose—adjust the seasonings, sweeteners, and amount of pork to suit your taste. When cooking them for myself, I like them sweet and peppery hot. When preparing them for others, I have to be more considerate. That's what I mean when I say they are never the same twice in a row!

1½	cups	dried bean mixture	375	mL
8		whole cloves	8	
1		large onion	1	
¼	cup	molasses	50	mL
¼	cup	brown sugar	50	mL
¼	cup	maple syrup (optional)	50	mL
½	cup	ketchup	125	mL
1	tbsp	dry mustard	15	mL
1	tsp	salt	5	mL
1	tbsp	Worcestershire sauce	15	mL
½	cup	reserved bean water	125	mL
		Diced salt pork, bacon ends, or baked ham bones		

Soak beans by the Quick Soak method or the Slow Soak method, pages 5 and 6. After draining the soaking water off, cover with fresh water, bring to a boil, and simmer slowly until tender. Time will vary from 30 to 45 minutes. Navy beans generally take the longest to precook so check them. If they are tender and if the skin of a sample navy bean comes off when it's blown on, then all the beans should be cooked. Drain again and reserve ½ cup (125 mL) of the hot bean water.

Stick cloves into onion and put into the bottom of the bean pot, large casserole, or slow cooker. Add remaining ingredients to beans and pour over onion. Tuck in meat. At this point, you should be able to see liquid through the bean mixture. Add reserved bean liquid, and some fresh

51

water or tomato juice or broth if necessary. Just be sure there's some liquid showing through before you cover the beans and bake for 6 to 9 hours at 250°F (120°C). If you're using a slow cooker, check your manual to see how long baked beans should take. Add more liquid if the mixture gets dry during the cooking process and stir occasionally so that beans are well mixed with the sauce. Uncover for the last half hour. Taste and adjust seasonings.

Serves 4 to 6 hearty eaters. Happy eaters, too!

Jean's Beans on the Trail

I have always been interested in pioneer recipes, and this method of cooking Jean's Beans would have suited those chuckwagon cooks on the cattle trails.

Prepare the above recipe to the final baking stage. Then dig a hole at least 4 inches (10 cm) deeper than the heavy iron pot—which it should be if it's going to be put to this use! Prepare enough coals to have a good layer underneath the pot and on top of it. Put the bottom layer of hot coals into the pit, then lower the pot in, covering the lid with a layer of foil to ensure that no dirt gets in. Cover with remaining coals and bury under at least 3 inches (8 cm) of dirt. Bake in the pit for at least 4 hours, watching that the dirt stays in place to hold in all the heat.

Sufferin' Settlers' Succotash

First the explorers and later the settlers learned from native Americans how to combine beans and corn into a dish called *Sukquttahhsh*, now known as Succotash. It was made from fresh beans (generally lima) and fresh corn (generally white), but it could also be made from dried beans and corn. The following modern version can be made quickly from canned products. Incidentally, try the hickory smoke, in either liquid or powdered form. It's optional in this recipe but it adds a very interesting taste.

1	can (19 oz/540 mL) hominy or white corn	1
2	cans (14 oz/398 mL each) lima beans	2
2	cans (14 oz/398 mL each) creamed corn	2
	Hickory smoke flavoring (optional)	

Note: For a meal in one, leftover chicken or turkey or strips of corned beef may be added to the mixture before heating.

Drain hominy and beans, then mix with creamed corn. Season to taste with hickory smoke. Heat and serve. Makes enough for 8.

Beef Shank and Trail Beans

The chuckwagon cook was a very important part of ranching in the early days. He—for it was usually a he—had limited supplies, limited equipment but still had to turn out hearty, healthy meals. Needless to say, beans were a mainstay. Often the beans had to be served up absolutely unadorned, but now and then, they'd get a piece of beef and then it would be beans and beef for supper. This is a modern variation.

½	lb	dried small lima beans	250	g
½	lb	dried pinto or kidney beans	250	g
3		slices bacon	3	
5	lb	beef shank	2.5	kg
2	tbsp	flour	30	mL
2		large onions	2	
2		cans (19 oz/540 mL each) tomatoes	2	
1	tbsp	salt	15	mL
½	tsp	freshly ground pepper	2	mL
¼	tsp	crushed red pepper	1	mL
1	tsp	dried thyme	5	mL
1		bay leaf	1	

Note: If the beef shanks are sold whole, get the butcher to cross cut each one into 3 or 4 pieces.

Prepare beans by either the Quick Soak or Slow Soak method outlined on pages 5 and 6. Once soaking process has been completed, cover beans with fresh water, bring to a hard boil for 10 minutes, then simmer for 20 minutes. Drain and reserve bean water.

Meanwhile, in a large frying pan, sauté bacon until crisp. Remove bacon and set aside. Coat beef shank pieces with flour and brown on all sides in bacon drippings, transferring them as they brown to a large baking dish or bean pot (if the opening is large enough to accommodate the beef pieces). Add drained beans to pot as well.

Chop onions and sauté in remaining bacon drippings. (Use extra vegetable oil, if needed.) Stir in tomatoes, salt, pepper, red pepper, thyme, and bay leaf. Stir well until tomatoes are broken up and whole mixture is boiling. Pour over beans and meat.

Cover and bake in a 325°F (160°C) oven for 1½ hours or until beans are tender. Stir occasionally and add more of the reserved bean liquid if the mixture seems dry.

Before serving, crumble bacon on top and allow to heat through. Serves about 8 hungry trail riders or maybe 12 pedestrians!

Boston Baked Beans with Brown Bread

The city of Boston has another name, Bean Town, dating back to the Puritans and their strict observance of the Sabbath. Because they were not allowed to cook from sundown Saturday to sundown Sunday, they made up big pots of beans and pans of steamed brown bread – enough to do them the whole weekend. Community ovens located in the cellars of local taverns were also available. The local baker would call on Saturday mornings to collect the family's bean pot, ready for baking, returning it hot and ready to use in the evening, together with a loaf of brown bread. Notice there are no frills in this version of the original recipe. It's as sensible and no-nonsense as those Puritan pioneers were!

2	cups	dried navy beans	500	mL
6	cups	water	1.5	L
1½	cups	reserved bean liquid	375	mL
¼	cup	brown sugar	50	mL
2	tsp	salt	10	mL
1	tsp	dry mustard	5	mL
¼	cup	molasses	50	mL
¼	lb	salt pork	125	g
1		onion	1	
		Boston Brown Bread (recipe follows)		

Prepare beans by either the Quick Soak or Slow Soak method, pages 5 and 6. To drained beans, add 6 cups (1.5 L) fresh water, bring to a boil, and simmer for an hour or until tender. Drain, reserving the liquid. Put drained beans into an old-fashioned bean pot or a new-fashioned casserole dish with a cover.

To 1½ cups (375 mL) of the bean liquid, add brown sugar, salt, dry mustard, and molasses. Pour over beans. Cut salt pork into pieces, chop onion, and add both to beans. Cover and bake in a 300°F (150°C) oven for 5 to 6 hours or until tender. Stir occasionally. If the mixture seems dry, add more bean liquid. Serve with Boston Brown Bread. Makes 4 servings.

Boston Brown Bread

Boston brown bread was originally served wth beans as a right and proper Sabbath meal. It can still be served that way, but it can also be served as an appetizer, as a snack at any time of the day, or as a delicious accompaniment to any number of main-course casseroles. Because it's steamed, it's lovely and moist!

This moist, quick bread is traditionally steamed in round cans, so find the size of can you'd like to use (the 19 oz/540 mL can is good or the slightly larger coffee cans). Remove the top completely.Grease the bottom and sides of the cans and line with waxed paper.

1	cup	rye flour	250	mL
1	cup	yellow cornmeal	250	mL
1	cup	graham or whole wheat flour	250	mL
1	tsp	salt	5	mL
2	tsp	baking soda	10	mL
¾	cup	molasses	175	mL
2	cups	buttermilk	500	mL
1	cup	raisins (optional)	250	mL

Note: The raisins are a modern frill, but they are a tasty addition.

Mix dry ingredients together. Make a well in the center and add, all at once, molasses and buttermilk. Stir well. Add raisins, if using.

Fill prepared cans about three-quarters full and cover tightly with foil, fastening it down with elastics or string to keep it in place. Place tins on a rack in a large kettle. A canner or Dutch oven would work well. Pour boiling water into the pot so that the water comes approximately halfway up the cans. Cover the pot tightly and let bread steam for 2½ to 3 hours, adding more boiling water as needed to keep the level in the pot at the halfway mark.

Test bread for doneness as you would a cake, with a toothpick or a cake tester. When done, remove foil and let bread cool slightly in the cans. Then remove from cans and serve hot. Nice with the beans as the Puritans intended but also wonderful with cream cheese, flavored butters, or cheese, or as an accompaniment to any number of main-course casseroles. Makes two 1 lb (500 g) loaves—two of the 19 oz (540 mL) cans would do.

Weiners and Beans

Here are two variations on an old favorite especially for the camping crowd. After all, what is it they sing at camp? "Weiners and beans, weiners and beans, that's all they feed me, weiners and beans."

Cheesy Hot Dog with Beans

You'll need one hot dog bun, one weiner, ½ slice of cheese, and approximately ½ cup (125 mL) of cooked beans for one serving of this casual treat. Heat the weiners by whatever method preferred—boiled or roasted over the campfire, or done in the microwave of the nearest recreational vehicle! Heat the beans at the same time. Split the bun and heat on the grill or campfire as well.

To assemble the hot dog, pile cooked beans on the bun first. Then slit the weiner lengthwise and put it on the beans. Tuck the cheese into the weiner and finish off with various garnishes, like ketchup, relish, mustard. Keep paper napkins handy and enjoy a delicious outdoors treat.

Round Dogs

Use hamburger buns this time and turn your weiners into "round dogs" by making a series of cuts along one side of the weiner. To keep the curl, it's best to heat the weiners in a frying pan or over a grill.

Assemble as above. Put heated beans on the bun first, then the round dog, then a slice of cheese (or a pile of grated cheese in the middle of the round dog), and finally the condiments.

Maple Syrup-Rum Baked Beans

To me, Madame Jehane Benoit will always be Canada's first lady of food. Whenever I want an idea for using Canadian food products, I can be sure to find answers in her books. She has many recipes for using pulses but this is my choice, and it is a great honor to be able, with her gracious permission, to include it in this book. It's been in her family for six generations. Her grandmother added the layer of apples to the original recipe, and her own granddaughter uses the recipe regularly.

4	cups	dried Great Northern or pink beans	1	L
		Rapidly boiling water to cover		
2	tbsp	molasses	25	mL
1	lb	slab bacon	500	g
1		large onion	1	
1	tsp	dry mustard	5	mL
1	cup	maple syrup	250	mL
1	tbsp	salt (coarse is best)	15	mL
4		apples, unpeeled	4	
1	cup	brown sugar	250	mL
½	cup	butter	125	mL
½	cup	rum	125	mL

Note: Navy beans could also be used.

Pick over beans and wash thoroughly in cold water. Place in a large pot and add boiling water to cover. Stir in molasses. Cover and let stand 1 hour. Uncover; bring to a rapid boil in the same water. Cover again and simmer for about 1½ hours or until beans are just starting to become

56

tender. Time will vary according to the age and dryness of the beans. Never add salt at this stage as it hardens the beans.

Meanwhile, slice bacon and use it to line the bottom of the pot, placing remaining slices here and there in beans. Then pour in beans and the water they've been simmering in.

Peel onion but leave it whole. Roll it in mustard until all of the mustard sticks to it. Then bury it in the middle of the beans. Pour maple syrup over beans and meat, and sprinkle with salt. Cover. Slow bake 4 to 5 hours in a 325°F (160°C) oven. After 3 to 4 hours, stir. If the top is dry, add hot water slowly. Return to oven.

Core apples and leave whole, if possible. In the last hour of cooking, uncover beans and place apples on top, as close together as possible. If the opening of the pot is larger than 4 whole apples will cover, then cut the apples in half. Cream together brown sugar and butter. Spread on top of apples. Leave cover off and bake beans for another hour or so. As beans finish baking, the apple cover forms a delicious topping.

Pour the rum slowly on top of apples just before serving. Serve a portion of apple with each serving of beans. Serves 10 to 12.

Ginger Peachy Bean Pot

This recipe comes from Carolann Johnson who kept me on the straight and narrow while we did the television show "Town and Country Cooking." She has a young family and a busy life so she specializes in "quick, easy and very, very good" . . . like this update of baked beans.

2		cans (14 oz/398 mL each) pork and beans	2	
8		gingersnaps, crushed	8	
¼	cup	ketchup	50	mL
2	tbsp	molasses	25	mL
½	tsp	salt	2	mL
1		can (14 oz/398 mL) peach slices, drained	1	
1		can (12 oz/340 g) luncheon meat	1	

Note: You could substitute 1½ to 2 cups (375 to 500 mL) leftover ham, roast pork, or roast beef for the luncheon meat.

Combine beans, gingersnaps, ketchup, molasses, and salt. Place half the mixture in a 2 quart (2 L) casserole. Arrange peach slices over the bean mixture. Top with remaining mixture. Cut meat into slices or strips and place atop beans. Cover and bake in a 325°F (160°C) oven for 45 minutes. Uncover and bake another 15 minutes, or until bubbling and done. Serves 6 quite willingly!

Edmonton Klondike Beans

Every summer, the city of Edmonton dresses up to the nines, 1890s style, to celebrate the annual festival known as Klondike Days. Naturally, Edmontonians have to expect company, and one lady I know relies on this bean recipe to get her through the festivities. A light and creamy concoction, it can be made ahead of time and, most important, it can easily be stretched.

3		yellow onions, sliced	3	
2		cloves garlic, minced	2	
¼	cup	salad oil	50	mL
1		can (14 oz/398 mL) red kidney beans	1	
2		cans (14 oz/398 mL each) small green lima beans	2	
2		cans (14 oz/398 mL each) pork and beans	2	
¾	cup	brown sugar	175	mL
¼	cup	vinegar	50	mL
½	cup	ketchup	125	mL
1	tsp	dry mustard	5	mL
1	tsp	salt	5	mL

Note: This recipe doesn't call for bacon, but it could easily be added, in which case you'd fry the bacon (anywhere from ½ lb to 1 lb/250 to 500 g) until crisp and then use the bacon drippings rather than the salad oil as listed above.

Sauté onions and garlic in salad oil (or bacon drippings) until transparent. Drain kidney beans and lima beans but leave sauce on pork and beans. Mix beans with onion and garlic, bacon (if you're using it), and the remaining ingredients. Put into a bean pot or large casserole. At this point, the mixture could be refrigerated until 1¼ hours before serving.

To finish, cover and bake in a 350°F (180°C) oven for 30 minutes. Remove cover and bake for an additional 45 minutes. Makes 8 generous servings.

In China, during the Han Dynasty, third century B.C. to A.D. 124, a total of eighteen different kinds of beans were cultivated in the coastal region of Hangchow. Later, the soybean and its derivatives were the staples of the poorer classes.

Grandma Rees's Baked Brown Beans

The Calgary Stampede is a made-to-order occasion for baked beans and Wild West shenanigans. These baked beans, with their touch of liquid smoke, are reminiscent of the food and atmosphere of the cattle round-ups from which rodeos originated.

¼	lb	salt pork or bacon	125	g
3		medium onions	3	
4	cups	canned brown beans	1	L
⅓	cup	brown sugar	75	mL
½	cup	ketchup	125	mL
½	cup	prepared mustard	125	mL
		Dash of liquid smoke (optional)		
¼	lb	sliced bacon	125	g

Cut salt pork into chunks and fry until crisp. Remove from frying pan with a slotted spoon and set aside. Chop onions finely and sauté in drippings until transparent.

In a bowl, mix together beans, brown sugar, ketchup, mustard, and liquid smoke (if using). Add cooked meat and onions. Put everything into a large casserole, cover with bacon slices, and bake in a 325°F (160°C) oven for 2 hours. Serves 10.

This dish can be prepared in advance, then reheated. The flavors seem to get even better as they have a chance to blend.

Rummy Baked Beans

Rum serves beans well, but then there are people who would say that rum serves a lot of things well! This is a quick and easy—not to mention delicious—version of baked beans.

4		cans (14 oz/398 mL each) baked beans	4	
¼	cup	molasses	50	mL
¼	cup	rum	50	mL
2	tbsp	brown sugar	30	mL
1½	tsp	dry mustard	7	mL
2	tbsp	onion flakes	30	mL
2	tbsp	ketchup	25	mL
½	tsp	ginger powder	2	mL

Place beans in an ungreased shallow 3 quart (3 L) casserole dish and stir in remaining ingredients. Bake, uncovered, in a 350°F (180°C) oven for about an hour, stirring occasionally. When beans are crusty and bubbly, serve to 8 to 10 appreciative people!

Bunny's Baked Beans

Bunny Barss included this interesting variation on baked beans in *Come 'n Get It*, her cookbook about food in the early ranching days. The beans get a deep brown color and a good bit of flavor from the black coffee.

2½	cups	dried navy beans	625	mL
½	cup	brown sugar	125	mL
½	cup	molasses	125	mL
¼	cup	black coffee	50	mL
¼	cup	stewed tomatoes	50	mL
2	tsp	dry mustard	10	mL
2	tsp	salt	10	mL
½	lb	salt pork or side bacon	250	g
		Water to cover		

Note: If you don't have any coffee made up, you could use ¼ tsp (1 mL) instant coffee dissolved in ¼ cup (50 mL) water.

Prepare beans according to either of the methods outlined on pages 5 and 6. Once they've been drained of the first soaking water, add fresh water to cover and boil until tender, about an hour. Drain again.

Place beans in a bean pot or casserole dish. Add sugar, molasses, coffee, tomatoes, mustard, and salt. Cube salt pork or side bacon and add to beans. Cover with water. Bake, uncovered, in a 300°F (150°C) oven for 5 to 6 hours. Check occasionally and add more water when necessary. Makes 6 servings.

No Fuss, Quick-and-Easy Beans

Here is a basic recipe for quick and easy beans! The long, slow cooking process helps to blend the flavors, but it can be dispensed with if you are in a hurry or if you are cooking over a campfire.

2	tbsp	bacon fat or oil	25	mL
1		large onion, sliced	1	
2		cans (14 oz/398 mL each) baked beans	2	
¼	cup	fancy molasses	50	mL
2		cans (14 oz/398 mL each) tomatoes	2	
1		can (14 oz/398 mL) tomato sauce	1	
1	tsp	dry mustard	5	mL
1	tsp	salt	5	mL

Notes: You could use 4 cups (1 L) cooked beans in place of the canned beans. You could also add meat of some sort to this mixture—leftover ham bones, bacon ends, or up to ¼ lb (125 g) salt pork.

In the bacon fat or oil, sauté onion briefly. Then add to remaining ingredients in a bean pot or large casserole with a lid. If using bacon or salt pork, leave it in a chunk, slashed to allow the flavors to blend, or cut it up into smaller pieces. If adding a ham bone, tuck it into the pot. Bake in a 300°F (150°C) oven, covered, for 2 to 3 hours. Makes 8 servings.

If you're in a hurry or doing these beans over a campfire perhaps, fry bacon or salt pork until crispy, add onion to fat, and fry until golden. Add remaining ingredients and bring to a bubbling boil over medium heat or coals, stirring gently now and then to mix well, then serve immediately.

Hurry-Up Baked Beans for a Bunch

This pot of beans will taste as good (almost) as beans made from scratch. Try it when unexpected company arrives, or when you just haven't time to work from scratch. Be sure to keep a variety of canned beans on your emergency shelf to be able to whip this up when needed.

½	lb	bacon or ham	250	g
4		onions, cut into rings	4	
1	cup	brown sugar	250	mL
2	tbsp	molasses	25	mL
2	tsp	dry mustard	10	mL
½	cup	vinegar	125	mL
		Garlic salt to taste		
1		can (14 oz/398 mL) kidney beans	1	
1		can (14 oz/398 mL) garbanzo beans	1	
1		can (14 oz/398 mL) pork and beans	1	
1		can (14 oz/398 mL) cut green beans	1	
1		can (14 oz/398 mL) cut yellow beans	1	

Note: Sometimes beans are available only in the 19 oz (540 mL) size. Never fear. This will work just as well. Don't buy the French-style green beans. Get the plain cut ones.

Cut up bacon or ham and brown in a frying pan. Remove meat with a slotted spoon and add onion rings to the fat remaining in the pan. Cook until soft. Add a bit of oil if the meat didn't produce much fat. Remove onions and set aside with the meat. To the fat remaining, add brown sugar, molasses, mustard, vinegar, and garlic salt. Stir and simmer for 20 minutes.

Place beans, meat, and onions in a large bean pot or casserole dish. Pour sauce over all, mix well, cover, and bake in a 350°F (180°C) oven for at least an hour. Serve with home-baked rolls or crusty buns. At least 12 people will go home happy!

Tex-Mex Chili con Carne (Beanless)

2	lb	lean beef	1	kg
⅓	cup	shortening	75	mL
2		hot red peppers	2	
4		cloves garlic, crushed	4	
¼	cup	chili powder	50	mL
2	tbsp	fresh oregano	30	mL
2	tsp	cayenne pepper	10	mL
1	tbsp	salt	15	mL
1	tsp	pepper	5	mL
2	tbsp	flour	30	mL
1	tbsp	brown sugar	15	mL
1	tbsp	cider vinegar	15	mL
2	cups	cold water	500	mL
		Beans to serve with the chili		
		Raw chopped onion, just in case you need more heat!		

Notes: The best shortening to use is lard. You may make this chili hotter or cooler by adjusting the amount of red pepper and chili powder used. Take care when using hot red peppers. They can burn your skin. Chili powder already contains oregano and dried red chilies, so you may want to cut down on the red peppers and increase the amount of chili powder. Use your judgment here. You know best what your household will tolerate.

Chop beef into shreds or ½ inch (1 cm) cubes. Do not grind. According to the people who win at chili cook-offs, "real" chili never contains ground meat. In a large frying pan or Dutch oven, brown meat in shortening. Cut red peppers into little bits, retaining the seeds. Mix peppers and all remaining ingredients (except beans and onion) with 1 cup (250 mL) cold water. Add slowly to the browned meat. Cook on high heat for about 3 minutes, stirring constantly. Add the second cup of water. Turn heat down and simmer, uncovered, for at least an hour or until meat is tender. You can simmer for several more hours, if you wish, as long as you add water when needed. Prepare whatever beans you plan to serve with the chili.

Serve chili and beans with raw chopped onion and watch out for fires! More good accompaniments for beanless chili include sour cream, sourdough bread or muffins, cornsticks, green salad with tomato slices, sweet red and green peppers. Then, of course, there are those that say chili should always be accompanied by Mexican beer! Serves 6.

Extra-Special Chili con Carne (with Beans)

My personal "secret ingredient" in recipes for chili con carne is unsweetened chocolate, about one square for a recipe that will serve about 10 people. I grate it and mix it in with the peppers and other seasonings. Maybe I like the idea of adding chocolate because there was a time when women were not allowed to indulge in chocolate. In fact, only royalty or the higher ranks of clergy and military were allowed to have anything to do with it. Luckily, we can all enjoy it now.

2	tbsp	vegetable oil	25	mL
4		medium onions	4	
½	lb	sausage meat	250	g
2	lb	ground beef	1	kg
1		can (14 oz/398 mL) red kidney beans	1	
2		cans (19 oz/540 mL each) tomatoes	2	
1		can (5½ oz/156 mL) tomato paste	1	
1	tbsp	Dijon mustard	15	mL
1	tbsp	red wine or tomato juice	15	mL
1½	tsp	lemon juice	7	mL
1	tbsp	chopped fresh dill	15	mL
1	tbsp	chopped fresh parsley	15	mL
1		clove garlic, minced	1	
1	tbsp	chili powder	15	mL
2	tsp	dried oregano	10	mL
1	tsp	ground cumin	5	mL
1	tsp	salt	5	mL
1	tsp	freshly ground pepper	5	mL
1		can (14 oz/398 mL) pitted black olives	1	
1		square (1 oz/28 g) unsweetened chocolate	1	
		Water (up to 1 cup/250 mL)		

Notes: If you can't get fresh dill, use 2 tsp (10 mL) dried dill weed. Also, the addition of chocolate is strictly optional. If you'd like to leave it out, you'll still have a very fine chili.

Heat oil in a Dutch oven or a large heavy saucepan. Chop onions; add to oil and cook until tender and transparent, about 10 minutes. Crumble sausage meat and ground beef and add to onions. Stir until meats are well browned and no pink is left. Remove as much excess fat as possible.

Add remaining ingredients, except for olives, chocolate, and water. Stir well and simmer, uncovered, for another 15 minutes. Taste and correct seasonings. Cut up olives. Add to meat mixture along with chocolate (if used) and simmer another 5 minutes. Add extra water at this point if the mixture seems too thick. Serve piping hot to 8 to 10 hungry folk.

Good accompaniments for Extra-Special Chili con Carne (with Beans) would be chopped raw onion, shredded cheddar cheese, or chopped green chilies. This chili is also very good reheated, at which time you may have to add extra liquid again. The recipe could easily be doubled — or more — if you need to make chili for a crowd.

Lorraine's Chili

This is a recipe from *The Perfect Pulses* . . . cookbook put out by the Pulse Growers Association of Alberta. Lorraine Rea, who's with the Alberta Department of Agriculture, tested the recipes for the book, and I like her chili recipe a lot. It's simple without being dull — perfect after a day of cross-country skiing or hiking in the mountains — and it freezes well for reappearances.

6	cups	cooked red kidney beans	1.5	L
⅓	cup	butter or margarine	75	mL
4		medium onions, sliced	4	
2		green peppers, chopped	2	
1	cup	diced celery	250	mL
3	lb	lean ground beef	1.5	kg
2		cans (28 oz/795 mL each) tomatoes	2	
3		cans (5½ oz/156 mL each) tomato paste	3	
1	tbsp	salt	15	mL
1	tsp	Tabasco sauce	5	mL
2	tbsp	chili powder	25	mL

Note: You'll need 2½ cups (625 mL) dried beans to produce 6 cups cooked beans.

If using dried beans, soak according to one of the methods outlined on pages 5 and 6. Then cover with fresh water, bring to a boil, and simmer until tender. Drain.

Melt butter in a large saucepan. Sauté onions, green pepper, and celery until onions are transparent. Add ground beef and cook until meat loses its pink color. Drain off excess fat. Add tomatoes, tomato paste, and seasonings. Cover and simmer 45 minutes. Add cooked beans and simmer another 20 minutes or so. Serves 16 to 20.

The Easiest of All Chili con Carne

You can serve this quick and easy version of chili with some chopped red onion, shredded cheddar cheese, or chopped green chilies. It is, however, very good on its own.

2	lb	ground beef	1	kg
1		large onion, chopped	1	
1–2		cloves garlic, minced	1–2	
1–2	tsp	chili powder	5–10	mL
1		can (5½ oz/156 mL) tomato paste	1	
1		can (19 oz/540 mL) tomatoes	1	
1	cup	water	250	mL
		Salt and pepper to taste		
2		cans (14 oz/398 mL each) kidney beans, drained	2	

Note: If meat is very lean, heat 2 tbsp (25 mL) salad oil in a heavy Dutch oven or large frying pan before browning the meat. If the meat has enough fat, then never mind the extra salad oil.

Brown meat well, breaking it up with a fork and, if necessary, doing it in several batches. Browning the meat well gives the chili more flavor and adds good color. If there's not enough room in the pan for the next step, remove some of the browned meat. Just set it aside. Cook onion and garlic in the same oil, adding a bit if needed. Put cooked meat back in. Add chili powder, tomato paste, tomatoes, and water. Season to taste.

If time will permit, allow the chili to simmer, covered, for an hour or so. If mixture gets dry, add water or tomato juice. Then add kidney beans just before serving, heating everything together thoroughly. Makes 8 servings.

Main-Course Dishes with Meat, Poultry, or Fish

Oats, peas, beans, and barley certainly do grow . . . all over the world. That's why you'll find bean dishes wherever you go. It's been my pleasure to take part in a "bean stalk" these past few years, trying out pulse recipes from all over. In fact, I've been around the world in eighty ways, and then some.

Thus, this chapter contains international bean classics, favorites in other countries like Brazilian Feijoada Completa, South African Bredie, Cuban Moors and Christians, French Cassoulet, and Tunisian beef stew, just to name a few. Since beans have been part of the human diet for at least four thousand years, it's not surprising that they turn up in so many different forms and with so many different tastes.

Incidentally, all the recipes in this section combine beans with meat, poultry, or fish to produce main-course meals. The incomplete protein in the beans is supplemented by the protein in the meat, poultry, or fish, thus providing a low-cost and efficient source of complete protein. As it turns out, our foremothers and forefathers instinctively served up complete proteins without the benefit of scientific research. I can't emphasize enough that, used in the right combinations, beans are nutritious, economical, and good for what ails us.

The recipes in the preceding chapter recreated down-home Canadian-style beans, foods that bring back warm memories. The recipes in this chapter are for new times and new experiences. Adventure along with me!

Frejon, Fish Stew

It is traditional, on Good Friday, for Nigerians to turn their usual fresh fish stew into Frejon with the addition of a bean puree flavored with fresh coconut.

3	tbsp	peanut oil	50	mL
2		green peppers, finely chopped	2	
2		onions, chopped	2	
2		tomatoes, peeled and diced	2	
1	tbsp	ketchup	15	mL
1	tsp	cayenne	5	mL
1	cup	boiling water	250	mL
1	lb	fresh fish fillets	500	g
		Salt (optional)		
1	cup	shredded fresh coconut	250	mL
2	cups	cold water	500	mL
2		cans (19 oz/540 mL each) beans	2	
		Sugar (optional)		
		Instant cream of wheat (optional)		

Notes: Try to use fresh coconut, but if that's impossible you can substitute dry shredded coconut that's been soaked in enough fresh milk to cover for 6 hours in the refrigerator. Drain off the milk before using. You can use kidney beans, pinto beans, or black-eyed peas for this recipe.

Heat oil in a large saucepan and add green peppers, onions, tomatoes, ketchup, and cayenne. Stir constantly until vegetables are soft. Add boiling water and stir well. Add fillets, which may be seasoned with salt if desired. Simmer until fish flakes easily when tested with a fork.

Soak coconut in cold water about 30 minutes. Strain, squeezing out all possible water and reserving the liquid. Keep coconut shreds aside.

In a blender or food processor, puree drained beans until they form a smooth paste. Pour into a small saucepan and add the coconut water. Sweeten with sugar, if desired. (Nigerians prefer a very sweet paste.) Cook paste over low heat, stirring often, until it is the consistency of very thick soup. Take a taste. The coconut flavor should come through. If it's not strong enough, add a few of the reserved coconut shreds and cook a bit longer. Add the coconut-flavored bean paste carefully to the fish stew, trying not to break up the fillets. Thicken stew with cream of wheat if a thicker sauce is desired. Makes 6 to 8 servings.

Cassoulet

Originally a peasant dish, cassoulet has become the gourmet version of baked beans, with as many recipes as there are cooks and cookbooks! One version won a gold medal in the World Culinary Olympics. Essentially, a cassoulet is a combination of white beans, meats, spices, tomatoes, and onions. But it's the meat that causes the controversy. Some cooks insist that a proper cassoulet includes pork only; others say preserved goose (*confit d'oie*) or duck must be included; others put any kind of meat they've got into the mixture . . . and so on. But all that aside, cassoulet is a delicious way to serve beans. It takes a long time to make — it's best to prepare ingredients the day before you plan to assemble the cassoulet — but it's well worth it!

2	lb	dried Great Northern beans	1	kg
6		whole cloves	6	
2		onions	2	
2		cloves garlic, chopped	2	
2		carrots, sliced	2	
¼	lb	salt pork or bacon, diced	125	g
5		sprigs fresh parsley	5	
1		bay leaf	1	
½	tsp	dried thyme	2	mL
3	tbsp	vegetable oil	50	mL
1½	lb	pork, cubed	750	g
1	lb	lamb, cubed	500	g
		Salt and pepper to taste		
1	lb	garlic sausage	500	g
2		onions, chopped	2	
2		cloves garlic, minced	2	
1		can (19 oz/540 mL) tomatoes	1	
1	cup	dry white wine	250	mL
2	cups	meat stock or water	500	mL
1		duck or goose	1	

Topping

2	cups	white bread crumbs	500	mL
½	cup	chopped fresh parsley	125	mL

You may want to get the beginning and the end of this recipe started at once. In other words, put the beans on to soak using the Quick Soak method, page 6. At the same time, put the duck (or goose) in to roast. Once the fowl is cool, cut off the meat in good-sized pieces.

Now, back to the cassoulet. Once beans have been drained of their first soaking water, cover with fresh water and put back on the heat.

Poke whole cloves into onions and add to beans. Add garlic, carrot, salt pork, and seasonings. Bring to a boil, reduce heat, and simmer for about an hour or until beans are nearly tender. Skim off any foam. Remove parsley, bay leaf, and whole cloves.

In a large heavy frying pan, heat oil and brown pork and lamb, sprinkling with salt and pepper. Remove and set aside. Cut garlic sausage into ½ inch (1 cm) pieces and brown in the same pan. Remove and set aside. Add more oil, if necessary. Sauté onions and garlic until soft. Add tomatoes, wine, and meat stock. Simmer about 5 minutes, breaking up the tomato pieces as you stir. Return pork and lamb to the pan. Simmer, covered, until completely tender, anywhere from 1 to 1½ hours depending on the cut of meat. Test by tasting and simmer longer, if necessary.

Now begin assembling the final product. In a large heavy casserole, layer about one-third of the bean mixture, then half of the duck or goose meat, half of the meats in tomato sauce, and half of the sausage. Repeat layers ending with beans and a few sausage pieces on top. Add enough bean liquid to almost cover the mixture.

For the traditional crumb topping, mix up bread crumbs with parsley and sprinkle on top. Bake uncovered in a 325°F (160°C) oven for 1½ to 2 hours. As the crust browns lightly, break it into the beans with the back of a spoon and baste with the liquid in the casserole. Repeat several times through the baking process, leaving a final crust intact for serving. After initial baking time, let cassoulet stand in oven at low heat (200°F/100°C) for another hour. Or you could refrigerate your creation at this point and bring it back to heat when ready to serve.

Serve with lots of pomp and circumstance. Be sure your spouse doesn't invite the guests to have more "pork and beans," because this is a very special treat indeed! Serves 16 to 20 lucky people.

Ancient Egyptian priests were forbidden many foods, including fish and beans, which were considered unclean. Times have changed, however, and today Egyptians enjoy beans. One of their popular recipes, Foul, can be found on page 99.

Quick Curried Beans with Beef and Rice

This is an interesting combination of traditions: a little bit of curry to remind us of the Far East, a bit of cayenne to remind us of Mexico, and beans and rice used in such a way as to be reminiscent of countries all over the world.

1	lb	ground beef	500 g
1		medium onion, chopped	1
1		can (28 oz/796 mL) baked beans	1
1		can (10 oz/284 mL) mushrooms, drained	1
1	cup	cooked rice	250 mL
1	tsp	salt	5 mL
1½	tsp	curry powder	7 mL
		Dash of cayenne pepper	
½	cup	raisins (optional)	125 mL

Brown beef with onion in a large frying pan. Drain fat. Add remaining ingredients, taste to adjust seasonings, and heat through to serve. Serves 4 to 6 quickly and efficiently!

Feijoada Completa

Since Brazil is often called the "land of the bean," no worldwide collection of bean recipes would be complete without Feijoada Completa, Brazil's special party dish. Preparations should be spread over several days, and when the dish is offered it should be greeted with gratitude and eaten with due respect for the beautiful presentation.

As with many national dishes, it began as a hearty version of beans and meat—cured pork and dried or salted beef. For special occasions, more meat, vegetables, and fruits were added as the budget would allow. Today, Feijoada Completa, an ideal choice for a buffet-style meal, must still include the original smoked meats but now fresh pork and beef have been added and everything is arranged on a large platter around a sliced smoked tongue. The meat platter is glazed with a sauce containing pureed black beans. It's surrounded with bowls of black beans; rice; kale (or cabbage); slices of orange; sliced onions (or a sauce of onions, pepper, and lemon—recipe follows); and a bowl of toasted manioc flour (or farina), the latter being garnished with stuffed green olives and hard-cooked eggs cut in half lengthwise.

The following recipe is as simple as I can make it and still retain the essential parts.

1	lb	dried beef or corned beef	500	g
1		smoked beef tongue	1	
4	cups	dried black beans	1	L
½	lb	chorizos or hot Italian sausage	250	g
½	lb	salt pork	250	g
2	tbsp	butter or corn oil	25	mL
2		large onions, chopped	2	
2		cloves garlic, minced	2	
¼	cup	sausage meat	50	mL
3		hot chili peppers	3	
6	cups	hot cooked rice	1.5	L
1		head kale or green cabbage	1	
		Black Bean Glaze (recipe follows)		
4		oranges, sliced	4	
4		large, sweet onions, sliced (optional)	4	
		Toasted manioc flour or farina		
		Hard-cooked eggs and stuffed green olives		
		Onion, Pepper, and Lemon Sauce (optional, recipe follows)		

Note: Instead of hot chili peppers, you can use a pinch of cayenne pepper.

In a large pot, soak dried beef (or corned beef) and tongue in water to cover 5 to 6 hours or overnight. Prepare beans according to one of the methods outlined on pages 5 and 6. Place drained beans in a saucepan and cover with fresh water. Boil for 10 minutes, then reduce heat and simmer, covered, for 30 minutes.

Drain soaked meats. Cover with fresh water, bring to a boil, and simmer for 5 minutes. Drain again and rinse. Cover with warm water and simmer for 1 hour. Add chorizos, pricked all over with a fork, and salt pork. Simmer for 10 minutes. Drain and cool slightly.

Remove skin from tongue. Add to beans and bean water with dried beef, chorizos, and salt pork, still in whole pieces. Cover and simmer for 2 hours. Remove meats from bean pot and keep warm.

Heat butter in a frying pan and sauté onions and garlic. Add 1 cup (250 mL) soft beans (from the bean pot), ¼ cup (50 mL) sausage meat, and chili peppers or cayenne pepper. Mash and stir for 10 minutes. Reserve 1 cup (250 mL) of this mixture for Black Bean Glaze. Return balance to bean pot, simmering beans for another 30 minutes.

Prepare rice. Steam kale until tender but not mushy. Keep both hot while Feijoada is assembled.

Slice meats and arrange attractively on a large platter. Traditionally, the smoked meats would have been separated from the fresh meats by the tongue, which was sliced and arranged down the middle of the platter. Glaze meat with Black Bean Glaze and then serve beans, rice, and kale separately. Offer sliced oranges, sliced onions, and toasted manioc flour or farina garnished with hard-cooked eggs and stuffed green olives. Or you could make the Onion, Pepper, and Lemon Sauce to replace the sliced onions. Serves 12.

Black Bean Glaze

2	large tomatoes	2
3–4	hot peppers	3–4
2	cloves garlic	2
	Juice of 2 lemons	
½ cup	wine vinegar	125 mL
2	onions, finely chopped	2
4	scallions or green onions	4
6	sprigs fresh parsley, minced	6
	Pepper to taste	
1 cup	reserved bean and sausage mixture from Feijoada Completa	250 mL
	Salt and cayenne pepper to taste	

Note: You can use hot pepper sauce to taste instead of the hot peppers.

Peel, seed, and chop tomatoes. Mince hot peppers and garlic. Put all three into a blender. Add remaining ingredients, except for salt and cayenne pepper, and blend until smooth. Taste and add salt and cayenne pepper as needed. Sauce should be peppery. Makes about 3 cups.

Onion, Pepper, and Lemon Sauce

Use this instead of plain sliced onion as one of the side dishes to accompany the meat.

4	sweet banana peppers	4
½ cup	finely chopped onion	125 mL
¼ tsp	minced garlic	1 mL
½ cup	fresh lemon juice	125 mL

Note: Sweet banana peppers are available in bottles in red and yellow. Try using 2 of each color. The balance of the jar will keep indefinitely in the refrigerator.

Drain banana peppers and chop finely. Combine all ingredients in a bowl and stir until well mixed. Marinate, uncovered, at room temperature, for an hour before serving, or refrigerate, covered, for as long as 4 hours.

Moors and Christians

Combinations of beans and rice are found in many countries under a wide and wonderful array of names! This Cuban dish owes its name to the mix of races that have always been a part of Latin America's history.

10	oz	dried black beans	284	g
1		small ham bone or smoked pork hock	1	
1		clove garlic, minced	1	
1		bay leaf	1	
		Pinch dried thyme		
2		sprigs fresh parsley	2	
1	tbsp	vegetable oil	15	mL
1		onion, chopped	1	
1		green pepper, chopped	1	
1		tomato—peeled, seeded, and chopped	1	
1	tbsp	vinegar	15	mL
		Freshly ground black pepper to taste		
4	cups	hot cooked rice	1	L

Garnish

Sliced hard-cooked egg, minced green onions, and lemon wedges

Prepare beans by either of the soaking methods outlined on pages 5 and 6. Put drained beans into a large pot with ham bone or smoked pork. Cover with water and add garlic, bay leaf, thyme, and parsley. Simmer slowly for 2 to 3 hours or until beans are almost tender. This can take a long time so don't be discouraged. Keep at it until the beans lose their resistance! Remove the meat, cut into manageable pieces, and return to beans. Discard bone.

Once beans have been mastered, heat oil in a large skillet and sauté onion and green pepper until soft. Add tomato and vinegar and heat through. Add to beans. Add pepper to taste and simmer for another 30 minutes, just long enough to let flavors blend but not to lose the color of the vegetables.

Serve hot beans and meat on a bed of hot rice and garnish with eggs, onion, and lemon wedges. This is a very striking dish because of the color combinations. Make sure everyone admires your handiwork before you let them at it! Serves about 6.

Norma's Refried Beans

Every bean book has to tackle refried beans, but refried beans are one of those aggravating foods for which there doesn't seem to be a definitive recipe. However, in checking it out, it seems you should have pinto beans (sometimes mixed with kidney beans to make the color more appetizing), lard or bacon drippings for the actual frying (although I've used vegetable oil with good success), Tabasco sauce to taste, and finally, garnishes such as grated cheese, chopped green onion, and sour cream.

¼ cup	lard or bacon drippings	50 mL
2 cups	cooked pinto beans	500 mL
	Salt and pepper to taste	
	Tabasco sauce to taste	
	Grated cheese, green onions, sour cream to garnish	

Heat fat in a heavy frying pan. Add cooked and drained beans and fry over medium heat. Mash beans with a potato masher while they are cooking but don't puree them. They are not meant to be entirely smooth. Fry until all the fat is absorbed and beans begin to dry around the edges. Taste and add seasonings. When cooked, the inside part of the bean dish will be moist and the bottom slightly crusty.

You can serve them piping hot at this point, with cheese, onions, and/or sour cream available on the side. Or you could top them with grated cheese and let it cook in. Makes four ½ cup (125 mL) servings.

South African Bredie

I came back from a visit to South Africa with three new food words: *braai* meaning barbecue, *mealie-pap*, which is a cornmeal mush, and *bredie*, which originally meant spinach but now means vegetable. The meat suggested for this bredie is ribs or shoulder of lamb.

3		onions, sliced	3	
2-3	tbsp	oil	25-50	mL
1		2 lb (1 kg) deboned rib or shoulder of lamb	1	
		Salt and pepper to taste		
1	tsp	curry powder	5	mL
1		green chili pepper	1	
2		cloves garlic, minced	2	
2		cans (19 oz/540 mL each) beans	2	
		Lemon juice and sugar (optional)		

Notes: You can use either canned green chili pepper or fresh. As for the beans, use kidney, pinto, or fava beans, or marrowfat or black-eyed peas.

In a heavy roasting pan, brown onion in oil until golden. Cut meat into pieces. Sauté with onions until meat begins to lose its red color. Season to taste. Cover and simmer until meat is about half cooked, about an hour. Add curry powder, chopped chili pepper, and garlic. Continue cooking until meat is nearly tender. This will take from 30 minutes to 1 hour, depending on the cooperation of the meat. Drain beans, add to meat, and continue simmering until meat is fully tender and flavors are blended. Spoon off any excess fat.

Before serving, drizzle with lemon juice and add sugar to taste, if desired. This dish is good served with cornmeal muffins or fritters. Makes 8 servings.

Loubia, A Tunisian Stew

This North African country has its own way of seasoning bean dishes, and this ragout of white beans with meat and cumin is a good example. Loubia is often served with a fiery Tunisian ketchup called *harissa*, but I've used cayenne instead. It's still nice and hot!

3	tbsp	vegetable oil	50	mL
1	lb	stewing beef, veal, or lamb	500	g
½	tsp	whole cumin seeds	2	mL
6		cloves garlic, crushed	6	
1	tsp	ground cumin	5	mL
½	tsp	paprika	2	mL
½	tsp	ground caraway seed	2	mL
¼	tsp	cayenne	1	mL
2	cups	water	500	mL
¼	cup	tomato paste	50	mL
1	tsp	salt	5	mL
1		can (19 oz/540 mL) white kidney beans	1	

Notes: If white kidney beans are not available, look for Great Northern or cannellini beans. If whole cumin isn't available, use ¼ tsp (1 mL) crushed red pepper or increase the amount of ground cumin.

Heat oil in a Dutch oven or large saucepan and sear meat in it. Sprinkle cumin seeds over meat and continue to cook, stirring, until the seeds begin to snap. Add garlic, ground cumin, paprika, caraway, cayenne, and water. Stir in tomato paste and salt. Bring to a boil and simmer, covered, for 1½ to 2 hours.

Drain beans and add to the meat mixture. Simmer about 10 minutes longer. The meat should be fork tender and the sauce should be thick. Serve over rice or couscous. Serves 4.

Braised Shoulder of Lamb with White Beans

This recipe takes a long time, but the flavor of the sauce and the combined goodness of lamb and beans turns the whole combination into a gourmet treat fit for special guests.

1		4½–5 lb (2 kg) lamb shoulder	1	
¼	cup	vegetable oil	50	mL
4		carrots, sliced	4	
2		onions, sliced	2	
2		stalks celery, sliced	2	
2	cups	dry sherry or wine	500	mL
½	tsp	salt	2	mL
½	tsp	freshly ground pepper	2	mL
8		sprigs fresh parsley	8	
2		bay leaves	2	
¼	tsp	dried rosemary	1	mL
¼	tsp	dried thyme	1	mL
4		cloves garlic, minced	4	
3	cups	beef consommé	750	mL
		White Beans (recipe follows)		

Note: Have the butcher bone and roll the lamb shoulder. Keep the bones.

Preheat oven to 400°F (200°C). Put meat and bones into a heavy roaster and brown in oil on all sides until meat has a good crusty shell. This should take about 30 minutes. Remove meat and bones from pan and set aside. Reduce oven heat to 325°F (160°C).

Add sliced vegetables to oil in roaster and brown them for about 5 minutes on medium heat on top of the stove. Remove from pan and set aside with meat. Pour off any oil remaining in pan and discard.

Add sherry or wine to brown bits in roaster, scraping them loose; then simmer until liquid is reduced by half. Return meat, bones, and vegetables to pan. Add seasonings. Add enough consommé to almost cover meat, leaving only about one-quarter out of the liquid. Bring to a boil on top of the stove, then return to the oven and bake slowly, covered, about 2½ hours or until meat can be pierced easily with a fork. Turn meat occasionally and baste with the sauce while it is cooking.

When the meat is cooked, remove from pan. Strain the sauce and discard the bones and vegetables. Carefully skim the fat from the sauce.

76

Slice meat and arrange on a hot platter surrounded with White Beans. Pour a bit of the sauce over the meat and pass extra sauce in a bowl, if desired. Garnish with mint and serve to 8 to 10 people.

White Beans

2	cups	dried white beans	500	mL
3		sprigs fresh parsley	3	
2		bay leaves	2	
¼	tsp	dried thyme	1	mL
2		carrots, sliced	2	
2		onions, sliced	2	
2		cloves garlic, minced	2	
½–1	cup	sauce from lamb	125–250	mL

Notes: Put the parsley and bay leaves into a cheesecloth bag or metal tea ball, thus forming a bouquet garni that you can remove later. You can use navy or Great Northern beans in this recipe.

Prepare dried beans according to one of the methods outlined on pages 5 and 6. Put drained beans into a large pot, cover with fresh water. Add bouquet garni, thyme, carrots, onions, and garlic. Bring water to a boil, then simmer slowly until tender. Drain off any remaining water and remove the bouquet garni. When ready to serve, add enough of the lamb sauce to moisten the beans, and arrange them around the platter of sliced lamb.

Hoppin' John

This recipe is named for black-eyed peas, or black-eyed beans, or cowpeas—they're all the same thing—which are said to grow so fast in some countries that they "hop" right out of the ground. Besides being fast growers, in this dish black-eyed peas don't have to be presoaked, so it is faster to make than other combinations of rice and beans. In parts of the southern United States, a version of Hoppin' John is offered in homes, restaurants, even in bars, as a free lunch on New Year's Day. The tradition is thought to bring good luck. When this mixture first came to the States from its native Bahamas, the American cooks added tomatoes and cooked the beans and rice separately. However, the following is the original recipe.

1	lb	ham hocks	500	g
1		pkg. (10 oz/284 g) black-eyed peas	1	
1½	cups	uncooked rice	375	mL
½	tsp	Tabasco sauce	2	mL
1	tsp	chili powder	5	mL

Note: You could use 1 lb (500 g) bacon or salt pork instead of the ham hocks. If you do, just cook it along with the peas.

Parboil ham hocks for about 2 hours in a Dutch oven or large saucepan. Sort and rinse peas, discarding any that float. Add to ham and simmer for about an hour or until the peas are tender. Add rice, Tabasco, and chili powder. Adjust the amount of water at this point, bearing in mind that the rice needs three to four time its bulk. Bring to a boil, reduce heat, cover tightly, and let simmer for about 20 minutes or until rice is done and all liquid has been absorbed. Remove the meat from ham hocks and serve on the side. If using bacon or salt pork, leave it in the mixture. This recipe serves a lot of people and would be good for a large buffet.

Puchero, Argentinian Beans and Beef

It is only natural that Argentina would have recipes combining beans with its other well-known product, beef. This all-in-one-dish goes two steps further . . . and uses pork and whole kernel corn as well!

2	cups	dried garbanzo beans	500	mL
2	tbsp	vegetable oil	25	mL
½	lb	stewing beef, cubed	250	g
½	lb	pork, cubed	250	g
1		onion, chopped	1	
2		cloves garlic, minced	2	
4	cups	water	1	L
4		chicken bouillon cubes	4	
¼	tsp	cumin seeds or ground cumin	1	mL
1		dried red pepper	1	
1		potato, peeled and cubed	1	
1		tomato, peeled and diced	1	
1		green pepper, sliced	1	
1		pkg. (10 oz/284 g) frozen whole kernel corn	1	
1	tsp	salt	5	mL

Notes: You can use 2 tsp (10 mL) powdered chicken bouillon in place of the cubes. You can use ⅛ tsp (0.5 mL) cayenne pepper instead of the dried red pepper.

Wash and prepare beans according to either of the methods outlined on pages 5 and 6. In a large frying pan, heat oil and brown beef and pork cubes until no pink is showing. Remove meat and set aside. Sauté onion and garlic in drippings until onion is soft.

In a large Dutch oven or heavy saucepan, combine drained beans, browned meat, onion mixture, water, bouillon, cumin, and red pepper. Bring to a boil, then reduce heat, cover, and simmer until beans and meat are tender, about 1 to 1½ hours. Add potato, tomato, green pepper, corn, and salt. Simmer 30 minutes longer. Makes 6 to 10 servings.

Monday in New Orleans

Creole and Acadian cooks in the southern United States have traditionally used the ham bone left from Sunday's dinner to make this classic Monday dish of red beans, ham, and rice.

1	lb	dried red beans	500	g
1	tbsp	vegetable oil	15	mL
1	cup	chopped onion	250	mL
½	cup	chopped celery	125	mL
2		cloves garlic, minced	2	
½	tsp	dried thyme	2	mL
5	cups	water	1.25	L
		Salt and pepper to taste . . . depends on the ham		
½	tsp	Tabasco sauce	2	mL
1		large meaty ham bone	1	
2	cups	uncooked rice	500	mL
½	cup	chopped green onion	125	mL

Note: Try to get your ham bone broken into several pieces, partly to save space but also to allow the marrow to blend into the mixture. Old-timers claim the marrow is the secret to the success of this recipe.

Prepare your beans and soak by either of the methods outlined on pages 5 and 6. In large heavy pot, heat oil. Add onion, celery, and garlic, stirring until onion is tender but not brown. Add drained beans, thyme, water, salt and pepper, and Tabasco. Stir well. Bury ham bones in beans. Bring to a boil, reduce heat, cover, and simmer until beans are tender, anywhere from 1 to 1½ hours. Add boiling water if the mixture gets dry.

When beans are tender, remove about 1 cup (250 mL) and mash or puree in a blender. Return to the mixture and stir in well. Remove ham bones, cut off meat, and return meat to the beans.

Cook rice according to instructions on the package. Arrange hot cooked rice on a large platter, spoon beans on top, and garnish with green onion. Thus may you too enjoy Monday in New Orleans! Makes 8 servings.

Layered Rice and Bean Bake

Combinations of beans and rice turn up all over the world. This tasty dish using refried beans and green chilies originated in Mexico but is enjoyed everywhere it is served. It could be either a main course or an interesting contribution to a buffet table.

3		slices bacon	3	
½	cup	chopped onion	125	mL
1		clove garlic, minced	1	
1		can (14 oz/398 mL) refried beans	1	
3	cups	cooked rice	750	mL
1	cup	sour cream	250	mL
¼	cup	chopped canned green chilies	50	mL
3	tbsp	stuffed olives	50	mL
1	cup	grated cheddar cheese	250	mL

Note: This mixture has three distinct layers and looks most attractive baked in a clear casserole.

Cut bacon into small pieces and cook in a large frying pan until crisp. Remove and drain on paper towel, leaving 2 tbsp (25 mL) bacon fat in the pan. Add onion and garlic and sauté until tender. Add beans and stir until thoroughly blended. Stir in bacon bits. Spread mixture in greased 2 quart (2 L) casserole.

Mix rice, sour cream, chilies, and olives together. Spread over the bean mixture in the casserole. Spread cheese over the top. Bake, uncovered, in a 350°F (180°C) oven for 45 minutes or until cheese melts and bottom layers are heated through. Serves 4 to 5.

Irish Pease Pudding

There really was a pease porridge hot, pease porridge cold, pease porridge in the pot nine days old. It used to be a regular feature of menus in the British Isles, a favorite it is said, of King Edward VII, who was known for his love of good food. Original pease porridge recipes called for whole dried peas, which made for a lot of work and a long cooking time. The following is an easier method, with the same old-fashioned taste.

4	cups	dried yellow or green split peas	1	L
		Bouquet garni (see next page)		
1		egg	1	
2	tbsp	butter or margarine	25	mL
		Salt and pepper to taste		

Note: To make the bouquet garni, tie 3 sprigs of parsley, 1 bay leaf, and ½ tsp (2 mL) thyme in cheesecloth or place in a metal tea ball. You can also include 1 chopped medium yellow onion. Although the onion is not traditional, it does add extra flavor.

Rinse and pick over split peas. Cover with cold water, add bouquet garni, and bring to a boil. Reduce heat and simmer until peas are tender but not mushy. Drain peas well, then put through a food mill or puree in a blender or food processor.

Beat egg and add to peas with butter and salt and pepper to taste. Beat this mixture very well (old recipes say for at least 10 minutes), then pour into a well-floured pudding cloth, or use several thicknesses of cheesecloth, which can be discarded later. Tie the bag loosely to allow peas to swell, then drop bag into boiling water to cover and simmer for about 1 hour. Turn out on a hot platter and serve with additional melted butter. Serves 8 to 10 generously.

You could add your bundle of peas to any mixture of meat and vegetables you have simmering on the stove. After being chilled, any leftovers will slice and can be browned in hot oil and served up something like pancakes.

A Roundup Dinner!

This hearty variation on corned beef and cabbage takes on new flavor and extra goodness with the addition of split yellow peas. Not for those with dainty appetites, this pease porridge combination would be a welcome sight after a day of strenuous work . . . or play!

4	lb	corned beef	2	kg
8	oz	dried split yellow peas	250	g
6		potatoes, peeled and quartered	6	
6		carrots, scraped and halved	6	
1		turnip, peeled and cut into wedges	1	
1		cabbage, cut into wedges	1	
¼	cup	butter	50	mL
		Salt and pepper to taste		

Rinse meat under cold water, then cut into 2 inch (5 cm) cubes, discarding any large pieces of fat. Place into a large soup pot or Dutch oven and cover completely with water.

Wash and sort through peas. Put into a cotton bag or on several layers of cheesecloth, allowing room for expansion. Tie bag closed and place on top of the meat layer in the pot. Bring to a boil and let simmer for about 2½ hours. Remove any scum that forms in the first part of cooking. Add potatoes, carrots, and turnips to the meat pot. Cook about 15 minutes or until vegetables are almost done.

Remove the bag of peas and set aside. Add cabbage to the meat mixture. By this time, the liquid will have reduced, so the vegetables will be steamed rather than boiled, thus retaining even more of their original goodness. Steam cabbage with the rest of the meat and vegetables about 10 minutes, just enough to soften the leaves but not so much that the wedges lose their shape.

While cabbage cooks, empty peas into a small casserole dish, add butter, and mash well, seasoning to taste. Keep hot while removing meat and vegetables to a large platter for serving. Keep both elements of this meal as hot as possible. Pass the mustard and wait for the compliments! Serves 6 to 8.

Here Today, Gone to Maui

With so many Westerners spending the winter months in Hawaii, I was bound to find a baked bean casserole with a Hawaiian touch eventually . . . and sure enough, I did. With the beaches beckoning, no one wants to spend a lot of time in the kitchen and no one has to with this great addition to a luau!

4–5		green onions, chopped	4–5	
2		green peppers, chopped	2	
2		cloves garlic, minced	2	
2	tbsp	garlic-flavored oil (recipe follows)	25	mL
2		cans (14 oz/398 mL each) pork and beans	2	
1		can (14 oz/398 mL) pineapple chunks with juice	1	
½	cup	brown sugar	125	mL
2	tbsp	soy sauce	25	mL
1		can (10 oz/284 mL) water chestnuts, sliced	1	

Notes: You can use 2 cups (500 mL) diced fresh pineapple instead of the can of pineapple chunks. In fact, you could make pineapple boats to serve the beans in. Cut a medium-sized pineapple in half lengthwise; scoop out the flesh, saving it for the bean mixture. When the beans are cooked through, spoon into the pineapple shells and serve. For a heartier meal, add chunks of ham, roast pork, or cubed chicken to the bean mixture.

82

Sauté onion, green pepper, and garlic in oil. Add remaining ingredients and bake in a casserole in a 350°F (180°C) oven for 30 to 45 minutes or until heated through and bubbling. Makes 6 servings.

Garlic-flavored Oil

You can create a garlic-flavored oil perfect for recipes like this by peeling fresh cloves of garlic and storing them in a small jar of salad oil. That way, you keep the garlic fresh for a long time and always ready to use, plus you have a supply of garlic-flavored oil for frying or salad dressings.

Ginger Chicken and Chick-Peas

This chicken and chick-pea mixture is flavored with the spices usually found in commercially prepared curry powder. Thus, you can adjust the seasonings to suit your own preferences as you go along.

1		3–3½ lb (1.5–1.75 kg) frying chicken	1	
⅓	cup	lemon juice	75	mL
		Cold water to cover		
		Salt and pepper to taste		
1	tbsp	butter or oil	15	mL
2	cups	chopped onion	500	mL
¼	cup	minced fresh ginger	50	mL
1	tsp	ground cumin	5	mL
1	tsp	ground cardamom	5	mL
1	tsp	ground coriander	5	mL
		Pinch of hot red pepper flakes		
2	cups	cooked garbanzo beans	500	mL
2	cups	chicken broth	500	mL

Note: If you're buying canned garbanzos for this recipe, 1 can (19 oz/540 mL) would be about right.

Cut frying chicken into serving-sized pieces. Put into a bowl and sprinkle with lemon juice. Cover with cold water and let stand for 15 minutes. Drain and pat dry. Season to taste.

In a Dutch oven or large saucepan, heat butter and brown chicken on all sides. Remove chicken and set aside. Add onions to the pan, stirring over low heat until transparent. Add spices and cook for a few minutes more. Return chicken pieces to the pan. Add drained garbanzos and broth. Bring to a boil, reduce heat, cover, and let simmer for 30 minutes or until chicken is tender.

Serve over rice or noodles. Serves 6.

Seafood Chili

Today's dish is fish, according to the federal Department of Fisheries, and to back up their claim, they've come up with this recipe for Seafood Chili, an interesting combination of fish and beans. The fish is low in fat; the beans are high in protein, vitamin B, and iron. Who could ask for anything more?

1	lb	frozen fish fillets	500	g
½	cup	chopped onion	125	mL
½	cup	sliced celery	125	mL
½	cup	diced green pepper	125	mL
2		cloves garlic, minced	2	
1	tbsp	butter	25	mL
1		can (19 oz/540 mL) tomatoes	1	
1		can (14 oz/398 mL) red kidney beans	1	
¼	cup	cornstarch	50	mL
¼	cup	water	50	mL
2	tbsp	chopped fresh parsley	25	mL
¾	tsp	chili powder	3	mL
¾	tsp	salt	3	mL
¼	tsp	pepper	1	mL

Note: You may use cod, Boston bluefish, haddock, turbot, pickerel or walleye, northern pike, or lake whitefish.

Partially thaw fish fillets and cut in 1 inch (2 cm) pieces. Set aside.

In a large frying pan, sauté onion, celery, green pepper, and garlic in butter until tender. Add remaining ingredients except for the fish. Cover and simmer slowly for 30 minutes, or until thick, stirring occasionally. Add fish, cover again, and simmer 7 minutes or until fish is opaque and flakes easily.

Serve with a salad and buns or crusty bread. Serves 6.

Basque Garbanzo Casserole

This is the stew of Spain, a special lively blend of pepperoni, chicken, vegetables, and beans. It goes together quickly—especially if you use canned garbanzos—and it goes down very quickly as well!

½	lb	pepperoni	250	g
1–2	tbsp	vegetable oil, if necessary	15–25	mL
1		whole chicken breast	1	
1		leek, finely chopped	1	
2		cloves garlic, minced	2	
4		carrots, sliced across	4	

2	cups	shredded cabbage	500	mL
2		cans (19 oz/540 mL each) garbanzos	2	
1		can (19 oz/540 mL) tomatoes	1	
2	tsp	salt	10	mL
1	tsp	dried thyme	5	mL
½	tsp	pepper	2	mL

Note: If leeks aren't available, use green onions.

Cut pepperoni into chunks and sauté in a heavy frying pan for about 5 minutes. If pepperoni is dry, add a little vegetable oil. Remove meat with a slotted spoon.

Bone chicken breast, if necessary, and cut meat into 2 inch (5 cm) strips. Brown in the drippings from pepperoni and remove. Sauté leek and garlic in the drippings and then add carrot coins. Sauté together about 3 minutes. Stir in cabbage and cook 2 minutes longer.

Drain garbanzos. Mix with tomatoes, sautéed meats, vegetables, and seasonings. Put everything into a large casserole and cover and bake for 1 hour in a 325°F (160°C) oven.

A hearty, healthy meal. Serves 6 to 8 easily and nicely!

Swedish Beans, Bruna Bönor

Swedish beans are an interesting blend of sweet and sour, the sweet being provided by sugar and spices and the sour by apples and vinegar. They're a very tasty way to serve beans, especially if you make up the Swedish Meatballs as well.

1	lb	dried navy beans	500	g
1		stick cinnamon	1	
⅓	cup	brown sugar	75	mL
¼	cup	vinegar	50	mL
2	tbsp	golden corn syrup	25	mL
		Salt to taste		
¼	cup	molasses	50	mL
1	tsp	gravy coloring (optional)	5	mL
½	can	apple pie filling	½	can

Note: Swedish beans are always cooked on top of the stove, but you can use your judgment here and finish the beans in a slow oven if you wish. Navy beans sometimes take a very long time to get tender so allow yourself plenty of time to finish this recipe. Get the sweetened and spiced kind of apple pie filling.

Prepare beans according to one of the soak methods outlined on pages 5 and 6. In a heavy saucepan or Dutch oven, cover beans with fresh water. Add cinnamon, bring to a rolling boil, and simmer, covered, for about 1½ hours or until tender. The beans won't soften much after the sugar and vinegar are added so be sure they're on the tender side at this point.

Add brown sugar, vinegar, and corn syrup. Simmer for another 45 minutes. Taste and add salt, if necessary. Stir in molasses, gravy coloring (if using), and apple pie filling. Heat through. Watch that the mixture doesn't stick to the bottom since the liquid will have been pretty well reduced. Or, you could add all remaining ingredients when you add the sugar and vinegar and put the complete dish into a slow oven to bake, covered, for another hour or so.

These beans can be made a day ahead and reheated or frozen until needed. Serve with Swedish Meatballs or with roast pork, pork chops, or ham.

Swedish Meatballs, Köttbullar

These are the proper meatballs to serve with Swedish Beans, but they could also be made separately and served with heavy cream and snipped fresh dill, or a mushroom sauce, or whatever your imagination and cupboard has in store!

4		slices bread, no crusts	4	
⅔	cup	light cream	150	mL
½	cup	chopped onion	125	mL
1	tbsp	butter	15	mL
1	lb	lean ground beef	500	g
½	lb	lean ground pork	250	g
½	lb	lean ground veal	250	g
1		egg	1	
¼	cup	chopped fresh parsley or dill	50	mL
1½	tsp	salt	7	mL
		Dash each of ginger, nutmeg, and pepper		

Note: Swedish meatballs are best made with very finely ground meat. Ask your butcher to mix the three meats and put them through at least two more grindings. That way, you won't have to wrestle with a food processor when you start this recipe at home.

Soak bread in cream for about 5 minutes. Sauté onion in butter until soft but not brown. Combine meats, bread, cream, onion, egg, parsley or dill, and seasonings.

If you want to be completely authentic, you should now beat all the ingredients with an electric mixer, reducing them to a light, fluffy, smooth mixture. However, the meat tends to crawl up the beaters – unless you have a heavy-duty mixer – so you may prefer to beat by hand until the mixture is as smooth and fluffy as possible. Chill and then form into 1½ inch (3 cm) balls. Keep hands wet while working with the meat mixture to ensure nice round meatballs.

To cook the meatballs, you can either use the tried and true frying method – which is a bit fiddly and messy – or you can simply lay the meatballs on a foil-lined cookie sheet (dull side of foil up) and bake at 400°F (200°C) for 45 minutes.

Serve with Swedish Beans or your favorite sauce. Serves 8 to 10.

Steamed Sea Bass with Black Bean Sauce

The Chinese are noted for the beauty of their carefully prepared and flavored dishes and this one is no exception. Any other firm white fish may be substituted for the sea bass, but do not alter any of the other ingredients if you want to get the very best flavor.

1		sea bass, cleaned	1
1	tsp	salt	5 mL
2	tsp	fermented black beans	10 mL
1	tbsp	soy sauce	15 mL
1	tbsp	Chinese rice wine	15 mL
1	tbsp	vegetable oil	15 mL
½	tsp	sugar	2 mL
2	inch	piece fresh ginger root, peeled and cut into long, thin strips	5 cm
1		green onion with top, cut into 2 inch (5 cm) strips	1

Notes: Leave head and tail on the fish. You can buy fermented black beans in Chinese specialty shops. Instead of Chinese rice wine, you could use a pale dry sherry.

Wash fish well under cold water and pat dry inside and out. Make ¼ inch (1 cm) deep diagonal cuts, about 1 inch (1 cm) apart, along both sides. Sprinkle with salt, inside and out. Coarsely chop fermented beans and combine them in a bowl with soy sauce, wine, oil, and sugar, mixing well.

Lay fish on a heatproof serving platter that will fit inside a steamer. Pour the bean mixture over the diagonal cuts on the fish. Arrange ginger and onion in a crisscross design on top of the fish.

To cook, have enough water under the rack to come within 1 inch (2 cm) of the platter. Bring to a full rolling boil, then place the platter of fish on the steamer rack. Cover tightly and keep water at a continuous boil, replenishing it if necessary, steaming the fish for about 15 minutes or until it is firm and flakes easily.

Serve at once on the platter on which it was steamed. Serves 3 as a main course, or double that if it's part of a multicourse Chinese dinner.

Westphalian Blindhuhn

The Westphalian district of Germany is world famous for its pork, whose flavor originates, they say, from the diet of acorns that the pigs enjoy. Thus recipes from this district abound in combinations of pork, bacon, sausages, and ham with vegetables, including beans. This casserole combines beans with bacon or ham and vegetables and fruit. It has the interesting name of Blindhuhn or Blind Hen, interesting because there's nothing like a hen or even an egg in this recipe.

1	cup	dried white beans	250	mL
½	lb	ham or back bacon	250	g
4		cooking apples	4	
4		fresh pears	4	
2	cups	sliced green beans	500	mL
1	cup	diced carrots	250	mL
3		potatoes, peeled and cut into chunks	3	
		Salt and pepper to taste		

Notes: You can use sliced bacon, a piece of back bacon, or a piece of ham. Any fresh pears would be fine but in winter, the Anjou pears are the only ones available. Canned pears could be used if they're added toward the end of the cooking process. Otherwise, they'd get too mushy.

Prepare and soak the dried beans by either of the processes outlined on pages 5 and 6. Put drained beans into a large saucepan and cover with fresh water. Cut meat into about 6 pieces and add to the bean mixture. Bring to a rolling boil, lower heat, and simmer for about an hour, or until beans are nearly soft and tender.

When the beans and meat near the end of this simmering period, peel and cut the fruit into wedges. Add fruit and remaining vegetables to the bean mixture and simmer another 30 minutes, stirring occasionally, until the beans are fully cooked and the fruit and vegetables are tender. Adjust seasonings and serve like a main-course stew. This dish is good with brown bread and a green salad. Serves 6.

Crown Roast of Weiners
— with Champagne Baked Beans

Weiners and beans move into high society. Select an ovenproof container that will hold the finished beans in the centre of the crown for serving. It will also hold the crown upright while roasting. Allow 2 weiners per person, plus about 1-1½ cups (250-375 mL) of beans.

Using strong thread and a basting needle, run 2 rows of thread through the weiners, about 1½" (3 cm) in from each end. Depending on the length of the wieners, run a third thread through the middle, especially if using the European-style sausages. Wrap these around the container and place upright on a baking sheet. The centre container, if a can, may be wrapped inside and out with aluminum foil. Adjust the thread, and pull firmly around the centre, tie with a slip knot and adjust so that weiners are straight.

Prepare 1 recipe of Paul Warwick's Champagne Baked Beans and 1½ recipes of his accompanying Teriyaki Sauce recipe, on page 97. This is the sauce that turns these beans into something special. The sauce can also be used on chicken wings, or ribs.

For even more 'gilding of the lily,' during the final 10 minutes of heating the assembled crown and beans, brush the weiners with the sauce used in "Chicken in the Gold" — a favourite recipe from "The Best Little Cookbook in the West."

To serve — top each weiner with a paper frill, and pour the champagne. Campfire weiners and beans were never like this!

Gold Sauce

Mix equal portions of prepared mustard and honey, or adjust the proportions to suit your own taste — sweeter or hotter. To 1 cup (250 mL) of sauce add 2 tsp (10 mL) of curry powder (again this quantity may be adjusted up or down) mix well, and warm slightly to bring out the flavor of the curry powder. Brush liberally over the weiners, watching that they don't get too brown, as the honey is inclined to burn.

Vegetarian Dishes

More and more people are interested in vegetarian meals. I know as I talked to people about this book, many expressed the desire that I include a section on vegetarian dishes, and here it is.

We all have to have proteins, carbohydrates, and fats in our diets. Generally, we get our protein from meats, fish, dairy products, and eggs, all of which are complete protein foods. However, we can get some protein from other foods, foods that contain incomplete proteins. Enter beans, peas, and lentils.

Legumes contain anywhere from 10 to 40 percent protein. Soybeans, for example, are 40 percent protein, while lima beans are closer to 10 percent. But you can increase that percentage by combining legumes with other incomplete proteins or by combining them with a smaller amount of complete protein.

Old favorites like pork and beans are a combination of incomplete and complete proteins, as are macaroni and cheese, fish chowder, and chili con carne.

Combining incomplete proteins to make a complete protein is a little trickier, and if you want to cut out meat and dairy products entirely, you should get a book and study complementary proteins. But generally, to make a complete protein, you combine things like beans and rice, or peas and barley, or lentils and couscous—old favorites that we've been eating for centuries without knowing they were good for us.

Anyway, try some of the following vegetarian recipes. Some come from far away; some from close to home. All make the most of beans and are good for delicious, healthy eating.

Happy-Ever-After Lasagna with Beans

The original Happy-Ever-After Lasagna was an enormous hit in my first book and on our television cooking show, "Town and Country Cooking." Everyone wanted to know how to make lasagna without precooking the noodles. So I've included that most popular recipe in this book—updated with the addition of beans, of course, which means it's a vegetarian version. It's still tasty, still convenient.

1	tbsp	oil	15	mL
2		cloves garlic, minced	2	
1		small onion, chopped	1	
2	cups	cooked beans	500	mL
4	cups	tomato paste	1	L
1	tsp	dried oregano	5	mL
1	tsp	dried basil	5	mL
		Healthy dash of freshly ground pepper		
¾	lb	uncooked lasagna noodles	375	g
2	cups	ricotta cheese	500	mL
8	oz	sliced mozzarella cheese	250	g
¼	cup	grated Parmesan	50	mL

Notes: You can use red kidney beans or brown beans, canned or homemade. To make the lasagna even cheesier, increase the ricotta or mix it with some cottage cheese or mashed tofu. Additional vegetables such as mushrooms, eggplant, or zucchini can also be added to the sauce. Put them in when you sauté the onion and garlic. Instead of 4 cups (1 L) tomato paste, you could use part paste, part tomato sauce or juice.

Heat oil in a heavy frying pan. Sauté garlic and onions (and other vegetables, if you're using them). Drain and coarsely chop beans. Add to onions and garlic and cook for several minutes. Add tomato paste, oregano, basil, and pepper. Bring to a boil and simmer for 5 minutes.

To assemble the lasagna, spread about one-third of the bean sauce on the bottom of a 9 by 13 inch (3.5 L) pan or shallow casserole. Arrange a layer of the uncooked noodles along the pan to cover the sauce so that the noodles are touching but not overlapping. Use about one-third of the noodles. Cover this layer with half the ricotta, half the mozzarella, and another third of the sauce. Repeat with the noodles, ricotta, mozzarella, and sauce. Finish with the remaining noodles and sauce. Sprinkle with Parmesan. Cover pan tightly with foil. Bake in a 350°F (180°C) oven for about 1 hour or until the pasta is cooked. If there is too much liquid remaining in the pan, uncover and bake for another 10 to 15 minutes. Serves 6 to 8 as a main course.

Baked Beans with Chutney

To make these tasty beans qualify as a vegetarian dish, you'll have to find canned baked beans without pork added, or start from scratch and make your own baked beans. It's worth the effort because this is a very snappy version of baked beans.

2		cans (28 oz/796 mL each) baked beans	2
1	cup	chopped onion	250 mL
½	cup	fruit chutney	125 mL
2	tsp	dry mustard	10 mL
½	cup	honey	125 mL
½	cup	yogurt (optional)	125 mL

Stir first four ingredients together and pour into 2 quart (2 L) casserole. Pour the honey evenly over the top. Bake, covered, at 325°F (160°C) for 1 hour or until steaming hot. Uncover and bake another 30 minutes or so. Add yogurt about 15 minutes before taking the beans out of the oven. Yogurt highlights the spiciness of this dish; however, if you're not a yogurt fan, these beans are good as is.

Serve with a salad and a moist herb bread, perhaps the Dilly Bean Bread, page 105. Serves 8 to 10.

Baked Lentils with Cheese

The daughter of a friend of mine lives near an Amish/Mennonite settlement in Pennsylvania, and because her neighbors use them all the time, she has gained a new respect for lentils. I'm glad she shared this recipe with all of us because it's quick and nutritious, like all legume dishes, and most of all it's very, very tasty.

1	cup	dried lentils	250	mL
1	cup	water	250	mL
1	tsp	salt	5	mL
1	cup	canned tomatoes	250	mL
1	cup	chopped onions	250	mL
1		clove garlic, minced	1	
⅛	tsp	each sage, marjoram, thyme, and pepper	0.5	mL
1		bay leaf	1	
1		large carrot, sliced	1	
¼	cup	sliced celery	50	mL
½		green pepper, chopped	½	
		Fresh parsley (optional)		
1½	cups	grated cheese	375	mL

Note: Cheese may be cheddar, Swiss, or mozzarella.

Wash and sort lentils. Place them in a large casserole and add water, salt, tomatoes, onions, garlic, and herbs. Bake, covered, in a 375°F (190°C) oven for 30 minutes. Add carrot, celery, and green pepper. Bake, uncovered, for an additional 40 minutes. By this time, the water should be completely absorbed and the flavors mixed. Sprinkle parsley, if used, and cheese on top of the lentil mixture. Bake, uncovered, for 5 minutes or until cheese has melted. Serve with a salad and crusty buns. Serves 6 to 8.

Haitian National Dish, Think Warm!

Because Haiti was a colony of France until 1804, many Haitians speak French and use French cooking methods in their meals. Their native dish of beans and rice is served with almost every dinner. It has its own method of preparation and seasoning, making it different from other combinations of beans and rice.

1	cup	dried pinto or kidney beans	250	mL
1		clove garlic, minced	1	
1		onion, chopped	1	
1	tbsp	chopped fresh parsley	15	mL
⅓	cup	vegetable oil	75	mL
½	tsp	black pepper	2	mL
¼	tsp	ground cloves	1	mL
5½	cups	cold water	1.25	L
1	cup	uncooked rice	250	mL
2	tsp	salt	10	mL

Prepare beans according to one of the soaking methods outlined on pages 5 and 6. In a large frying pan or Dutch oven, sauté garlic, onion, and parsley in oil. Add pepper and cloves. Add well-drained beans to the mixture and sauté for about 5 minutes. Add water to beans, bring to a rolling boil, cover, and let simmer for 1 to 1½ hours, until beans begin to soften. Then add rice and salt and continue cooking, covered, until rice is done, about 14 minutes. (If the mixture gets dry before the rice is done, add hot water.)

Pour bean and rice mixture into a well-greased large casserole or baking dish and bake in a 250°F (125°C) oven for 30 minutes. This final baking seems to make the best of all the flavors.

Serve with other vegetables—hot or cold, a salad, and a steel band. Have fun! Enough for 8 to 10 hungry people.

Gado Gado, The Peanut Revisited

Some beans and peas look like nuts; the peanut is actually called a nut even though it is a member of the bean family. In fact, the peanut is known by so many names it's no wonder we're not sure of its botanical origins. In some places it's known as the goober; in others it's known as the groundnut or monkey nut. It often turns up in recipes chopped or made into a paste otherwise known as peanut butter. This recipe from Indonesia is a mixed vegetable and peanut sauce combination.

1	lb	fresh green beans	500	g
6		small new red potatoes	6	
1	lb	fresh spinach	500	g
1		green pepper	1	
1		bunch radishes	1	
1		cucumber	1	
1		can (14 oz/398 mL) bean sprouts	1	
1	lb	tofu	500	g
3	tbsp	oil	50	mL
3		hard-cooked eggs	3	
		Peanut Sauce (recipe follows)		

Notes: One carton (14 oz/397 g) frozen spinach may be used in place of the fresh. Fresh bean sprouts could be used instead of the canned bean sprouts, in which case you would lightly steam them before using. The tofu may come in a 1 lb (500 g) carton, a 19 oz (540 mL) can, or a 2½ by 2½ by 1¼ inch (6 by 6 by 3 cm) cake.

Trim beans, cut crosswise, and cook until just tender. Boil potatoes in their skins; cut in half if large. Steam spinach until wilted. Seed and cut green pepper into good-sized chunks. Trim radishes and cut in half if very large. Peel, seed, and cut cucumber into bite-sized pieces. Drain canned bean sprouts, add fresh water, heat, and then drain again. Drain tofu, cut into bite-sized pieces, then stir fry in hot oil until light brown on each side.

Arrange vegetables attractively on a large platter and garnish with hard-cooked eggs. Top with heated Peanut Sauce or pass sauce separately. Makes 10 to 12 servings.

Peanut Sauce

1		clove garlic	1	
1		medium onion	1	
½	cup	dry roasted shelled peanuts	125	mL
4	tbsp	smooth peanut butter	60	mL
½–1	tsp	crushed red pepper	2–5	mL
2	tbsp	shrimp paste	25	mL

2	tsp	brown sugar	10	mL
2	tbsp	lemon juice	25	mL
		Grated rind of 1 lemon		
1	cup	water	250	mL

Note: Shrimp paste is sold as *trassi* or *patis* in Oriental food stores. If it's not available, use anchovy paste or mashed canned anchovies instead. Anchovy paste in a tube will keep indefinitely in the refrigerator.

In a large blender or food processor, blend all ingredients except water until whole peanuts are partially chopped. Gradually add water until sauce is smooth and peanut butter is fully dissolved. Before serving, simmer for about 5 minutes. Makes about 1½ cups (375 mL).

South American Succotash

All succotash mixtures are pretty, what with the combination of yellow corn and green beans, but this one has an extra dash of color and taste with the addition of peppers, tomatoes, and squash.

½		medium onion, chopped	½	
1	tbsp	minced fresh parsley	15	mL
1		clove garlic, minced	1	
2	tbsp	vegetable oil	25	mL
2	tsp	paprika	10	mL
1		can (14 oz/398 mL) lima beans	1	
1		can (12 oz/341 mL) niblet corn, drained	1	
½		green pepper, cut into strips	½	
1		tomato—peeled, seeded, and cubed	1	
½	cup	cubed zucchini or yellow squash	125	mL
3	tbsp	reserved bean liquid	50	mL
		Salt and pepper to taste		

Notes: You can use fresh corn on the cob for this recipe. Just cut kernels off corn cobs, enough to make 1½ cups (375 mL). For the lima beans, you can use canned, as suggested, or frozen, or dried beans that have been soaked and cooked.

In a large frying pan or heavy saucepan, sauté onion, parsley, and garlic in vegetable oil for 2 minutes. Add paprika and continue to cook until onions are transparent.

Drain lima beans, reserving the liquid. Add to the onion mixture along with the remaining vegetables. Add just enough of the reserved bean liquid to moisten the mixture, then cover and simmer about 30 minutes until vegetables are tender. Uncover for the last 5 minutes to let liquid cook away. Season to taste. Serves 4 to 6.

Meatless Tamale Pie

This is a vegetarian version of the popular Mexican dish, topped with a crust made from cornmeal and cheese. The filling could be made up in advance and then kept until ready to bake, at which time, you'd add the crust and go to it!

Filling

¼	cup	chopped onion	50	mL
2		cloves garlic, minced	2	
1	cup	chopped green pepper	250	mL
1	tbsp	oil	15	mL
2	tbsp	tomato paste	25	mL
1	tsp	chili powder	5	mL
½	cup	water	125	mL
3	cups	mashed cooked beans	750	mL
¼	cup	sliced green olives	50	mL
3	tbsp	chopped fresh parsley	50	mL
		Freshly ground pepper to taste		

Crust

1	cup	yellow cornmeal	250	mL
1	tbsp	flour	15	mL
¼	tsp	salt	1	mL
1½	tsp	baking powder	7	mL
1		egg, lightly beaten	1	
½	cup	milk	125	mL
2	tbsp	oil	25	mL
2	tbsp	chopped green chilies	25	mL
½	cup	grated cheddar cheese	125	mL

Note: You may use kidney, pink, or pinto beans.

In a large frying pan, sauté onion, garlic, and green pepper in oil until onion is transparent. Add tomato paste and chili powder; then add water, beans, olives, parsley, and pepper. Simmer until heated through.

Grease an 8 inch (20 cm) baking dish or shallow casserole and spread the bean mixture evenly in the bottom. In another bowl, combine cornmeal, flour, salt, and baking powder. Add egg, milk, oil, and green chilies. Stir just to mix. Do not overbeat. Spread batter over the bean mixture, top with grated cheese, and bake, uncovered, at 400°F (200°C) for 20 minutes or until the batter rises and is golden brown. Serves 6 very well.

In ancient Greece, at the time of Socrates, an evening of games might end with wine and tidbits of dried fruit and grilled beans.

Champagne Baked Beans, page 97

Champagne Baked Beans

A friend of mine, Paul Warwick, is not only a wine educator and lecturer, but he's also a celebrity chef, showman, and most recently, a cookbook author. His book, *The Spirit of Cooking*, manages to slip something alcoholic into every recipe, often in surprising ways. The alcohol evaporates during the cooking, leaving just the desired flavor. This is Paul's favorite recipe for baked beans. To make this a vegetarian dish, find canned baked beans that haven't had pork added, or make your own from scratch.

2		onions, chopped	2	
2	cups	sliced fresh mushrooms	500	mL
3	tbsp	butter	50	mL
2		cans (14 oz/398 mL each) baked beans	2	
1	cup	grated cheddar cheese	250	mL
¼	cup	champagne	50	mL
		Teriyaki Sauce (recipe follows)		

Note: If you don't happen to have ¼ cup (50 mL) champagne sitting in the refrigerator, you could substitute red or white wine, or fruit juice, if all else fails.

Sauté onions and mushrooms in butter until soft. Mix gently with remaining ingredients and place in a large baking dish. Bake at 325°F (160°C) for about 30 minutes. Serves 6.

Paul recommends a dry red wine with this. I would prefer to drink the rest of the champagne!

Teriyaki Sauce

This is also a terrific sauce to use on chicken wing appetizers.

¼	cup	Kahlua or Tia Maria	50	mL
½	cup	maple syrup	125	mL
½	cup	ketchup	125	mL
2	tbsp	chili sauce	25	mL
1	tbsp	horseradish	15	mL
1	tsp	Dijon mustard	5	mL
1	tsp	Worcestershire sauce	5	mL
¼	cup	bottled teriyaki sauce	50	mL

In a frying pan, combine all ingredients. Stir until smooth, then reduce by half over high heat. Makes about 1 cup (250 mL).

Super Cabbage Roll with Beans and Rice

Cabbage leaves are wrapped around a lot of different fillings, then steamed, boiled, or baked. I have tried several versions: individual cabbage rolls, which can be time-consuming; larger variations; or even a whole cabbage hollowed out and then filled. This vegetarian version is somewhat similar to the whole cabbage idea, except that less cabbage is used around the outside of the bean and rice mixture. The whole thing is held together for baking by tying it in a cheesecloth or thin cotton square.

10		large cabbage leaves	10
1	cup	drained garbanzo beans	250 mL
⅓	cup	tomato paste	75 mL
1		egg yolk	1
½	tsp	chili powder	2 mL
½	tsp	ground cumin	2 mL
		Dash of salt	
1	cup	drained kidney beans	250 mL
1	cup	cooked rice (brown is best)	250 mL
½	cup	grated cheddar cheese	125 mL
1		can (4 oz/114 mL) green chili peppers, chopped	1
½	cup	chopped green onions	125 mL
¼	cup	shelled sunflower seeds	50 mL

Garnishes

Sour cream, sweet or hot chili peppers, tomato wedges, black olives, sprigs of fresh parsley

Note: You could make this recipe into individual cabbage rolls in the traditional way, if you prefer. You'd need more cabbage leaves and smaller ones.

To make this super cabbage roll, steam cabbage leaves about 5 minutes to soften them slightly. Remove the heavy veins and arrange 5 of the leaves in a circle on a dampened 20 inch (50 cm) square cloth or double thickness of cheesecloth, having the stem ends in the center and making an overlapping base.

Make a puree of garbanzo beans, tomato paste, and egg yolk. Add everything else except for the garnishes. Mix well. Mound the bean mixture into the center of the cabbage leaf arrangement. Cover with the other 5 leaves, stem ends in the center. Let the edges of the cabbage leaves drop down over the filling, then carefully pull up the cloth around the filling, bringing up the lower layer of cabbage around the edges of the filling. Tie tightly with string and, if necessary, trim off any excess cloth.

Place roll, tied end up, on a rack in a baking pan or casserole. Cover with lid or foil and bake in a 400°F (200°C) oven for an hour. Be prepared for the cloth to turn brown during the cooking time.

Remove from pan, unwrap the roll, and place on a serving plate. Try to show the best side of the cabbage roll! Serve with sour cream, sweet or hot chili peppers, tomatoes, olives, and frilly cilantro or curly parsley. Cut into 6 or 8 wedges to serve.

Foul, Otherwise Known as Fool

After learning that beans had once been a forbidden food for the high priests of ancient Egypt, I redoubled my "bean stalk" and located this modern Egyptian bean recipe. This would make a vegetarian lunch along with a salad and pita bread, or you could turn it into a nonvegetarian meal with the addition of cold cuts. Foul is the name of the broad bean used to make this dish in Egypt. The closest we have is green limas.

1		can (14 oz/398 mL) green lima beans	1	
3		onions, chopped	3	
1		clove garlic, minced	1	
4	tbsp	Garlic-flavored Oil (see page 83)	60	mL
2	tbsp	ketchup	25	mL
1	tbsp	flour	15	mL
4	tbsp	lemon juice	60	mL
½	tsp	paprika	2	mL
		Pinch of cayenne		
		Dash of salt		
		Liquid from canned beans (if needed)		

Do not drain lima beans. Put them and their juice on to heat while making the sauce. When beans are hot, drain and reserve liquid.

To make the sauce, sauté onions and garlic in hot oil until golden. Take off the heat. In a small bowl, mix ketchup, flour, and lemon juice until no lumps remain. Pour this mixture over onions and garlic. Return to heat and stir in paprika, cayenne, and salt. If the mixture is dry, add a bit of the hot liquid from the beans. Bring to a boil, stirring constantly, adding as much bean liquid as necessary to make a creamy sauce. Add heated beans and mix well, adding as much liquid as needed to make a smooth mixture. Stretch the liquid with boiling water, if necessary.

This dish can be served hot as a main meal or cold, arranged on a lettuce leaf or tucked into pita bread. It's a good accompaniment to daydreams about floating down the Nile! Makes 4 servings.

Dhal, Indian Lentil Puree

Highly digestible, dhal is a prime source of protein in Indian cuisine. The texture can vary from smooth soupy mixtures to dry pastes that are used to thicken sauces. Any number of spices may be added. Try the following version with rice as a main course or serve with pieces of chappatti (Indian flat bread) as a snack.

3	tbsp	Clarified Butter or Ghee (page 13)	50	mL
1		onion, chopped	1	
1		hot green chili pepper, finely chopped	1	
2	cups	dried lentils or yellow split peas	500	mL
4½	cups	water	1	L
1	tsp	turmeric or curry powder	5	mL
1	tbsp	crushed mustard seed	15	mL
1	tbsp	chopped fresh coriander	15	mL
		Salt to taste		

Note: You can use ½ tsp (2 mL) dried red chili pepper in place of the hot green chili pepper.

Make Clarified Butter or Ghee according to instructions on page 13. Melt ghee in a large saucepan and sauté onion and pepper. Add lentils and water. Simmer until tender, about 45 to 60 minutes. Add remaining ingredients and mix well. Serves 6 to 8 as a main-course meal.

Tri-Color Terrine

Dried beans and peas can be turned into a spectacular layered terrine, as appealing to the eye as to the taste buds. You can make individual terrines or one large one to be turned out and presented as guest of honor on a buffet table. Use layers of bean puree, alternating colors and adding more glamor and flavor with pimento, asparagus, or other cooked vegetables between the layers.

		Bouquet garni (page 30)		
2	cups	red Mexican bean puree, flavored with onion and garlic	500	mL
2	cups	white bean puree, flavored with chopped fresh dill weed	500	mL
2	cups	split green pea puree, flavored with 1 tbsp (15 mL) each chopped fresh dill weed and dried mint leaves	500	mL
2	tbsp	chili sauce or ketchup	25	mL
3		eggs, beaten	3	
		Well-cooked asparagus spears		

2	tbsp	heavy cream	25	mL
		Dash salt		
3		eggs, beaten	3	
		6 or 7 strips of pimento, or other cooked vegetables		
2	tbsp	heavy cream	25	mL
3		eggs, beaten	3	

Notes: If you find your split green peas don't seem green enough for the terrine, add a bit of green food coloring. I use Great Northerns for the white bean puree.

If starting from dried beans, prepare bean purees according to the instructions on page 8. To ensure a good flavor in the terrine, add a bouquet garni to beans as they cook. In addition, add onion and garlic to the cooking water for the red beans, to be removed before the beans are pureed. Add dill weed to the cooking water for the white beans, and dill weed and mint to the cooking water for the green split peas. If starting from canned beans, drain beans, rinse if necessary, and mash with a food mill or blender until very smooth. Keep each bean puree in a separate bowl.

Butter both sides of parchment paper (I save the wrappers from lard for this purpose) or wax paper and fit it into the bottom of a well-buttered baking dish. A 9 by 5 by 3 inch (2 L) loaf pan works well. Prepare another piece of paper for the top, buttered on one side only.

To the red bean puree, add chili sauce and 3 beaten eggs. Spoon into the baking dish, spreading the puree out evenly. Let sit a few minutes, then spread asparagus on top. To the white bean puree, add 2 tbsp (25 mL) cream, salt, and 3 beaten eggs. Spread carefully over the red layer without disturbing it. Top with pimento, evenly spaced, or any other cooked vegetable. To the green puree, add 2 tbsp (25 mL) cream and 3 beaten eggs. Spread over the other two layers. Cover with the buttered paper, buttered side down.

Place baking dish in a larger oven-proof dish. Fill to halfway up the terrine dish with hot water and bake at 350°F (180°C) for 1 hour or until terrine tests done with a wooden pick. If the pick doesn't come out clean, bake for 5 to 10 more minutes and test again.

Allow terrine to set for 10 to 15 minutes, then loosen top edge with a knife. Remove top paper and place serving dish over baking dish. Invert baking dish and platter together and carefully remove bottom paper.

Garnish terrine with fresh greens and serve hot or at room temperature as an appetizer, salad, or vegetable course. Pass your favorite red sauce or mayonnaise to complement the flavors. Makes 1 large loaf.

Ibiharage, Fried Beans

Not to be confused with Mexican refried beans, this is a spicy hold-onto-your-hat version of fried beans from Zambia.

3		onions, chopped	3
1		clove garlic, minced	1
⅓	cup	vegetable oil	75 mL
1		can (19 oz/540 mL) beans	1
1-2		chili peppers, chopped	1-2
2	tsp	salt	10 mL

Notes: Use canned lima beans, pinto beans, kidney beans, or black-eyed peas or start from scratch with dried beans. If you can't get chili peppers, use about ½ tsp (7 mL) crushed red pepper.

Sauté onions and garlic in hot oil until onions are transparent and soft. Add drained beans, chili peppers (or crushed red pepper), and salt. Continue to sauté for about 5 minutes more. Serve with hot breads as an accompaniment to other vegetables or salads. Serves 4.

Bean Salad with Rice

Putting beans and rice together in this salad is a good example of the whole being more than its parts! Beans by themselves are an incomplete protein. So is rice. But put them together and you create a complete protein. An all-round good deal!

1	cup	uncooked long-grain rice	250 mL
1		can (14 oz/398 mL) kidney beans	1
1	cup	broccoli flowerets	250 mL
½	lb	snow peas	250 g
1		pepper, red or green	1
4-6		green onions, sliced	4-6
2	cups	sliced fresh mushrooms	500 mL

Dressing

¼	cup	salad oil	50 mL
2	tbsp	lemon juice	25 mL
3	tbsp	vinegar	50 mL
2		cloves garlic, minced	2
1	tsp	dry mustard	5 mL
¾	tsp	dried tarragon, crumbled	4 mL
½	tsp	salt	2 mL
		Freshly ground pepper to taste	
		Greens to line salad bowl or platter	
		Cherry tomatoes to garnish	

Note: Rice may be either white or brown.

Cook rice according to package instructions. Don't add any butter. While rice cooks, prepare remaining ingredients. Drain and rinse canned beans. Steam broccoli for 5 minutes. Top, tail, and remove strings from snow peas. Cut green or red pepper into strips. Slice onions. Combine vegetables, including mushrooms, in a large bowl.

In a jar with a secure screw top, combine oil, lemon juice, vinegar, garlic, mustard, tarragon, and salt and pepper. Shake well and pour over the rice and vegetable mixture. Toss and refrigerate until ready to serve.

At serving time, cover a large bowl or platter with fresh greens, pile on the salad, and surround it with halved cherry tomatoes. It will look like a million bucks! Makes 8 large servings.

Bean Sauce with Rice

This is a very quick dish. You can make the sauce while the rice cooks and, voilà, supper in minutes! It's even faster if you happen to have 3 cups (750 mL) of rice already cooked.

1	cup	uncooked rice	250	mL
1	tbsp	vegetable oil	15	mL
1		large onion, chopped	1	
2		cloves garlic, minced	2	
2		fresh tomatoes, diced	2	
1		small zucchini, chopped	1	
½	tsp	dried oregano	2	mL
1		can (19 oz/540 mL) cooked beans	1	
		Salt and pepper to taste		
1	cup	grated cheddar cheese	250	mL

Note: Beans may be kidney, pinto, or garbanzo.

Cook rice according to the instructions on the package and keep warm until the sauce is cooked.

Heat oil in a large frying pan. Sauté onion and garlic until onion is transparent. Add tomatoes, zucchini, and oregano. Cover and simmer for about 5 minutes or until the vegetables are just tender. Drain beans and rinse. Add them to the frying pan. Simmer, stirring occasionally, until heated through. Season to taste.

To serve, spoon the sauce over the hot rice and sprinkle with grated cheese. Serves 4.

Breads

Bread and beans have been hand-in-hand partners for centuries. The traditional Boston Brown Beans were baked in community ovens along with the baker's more usual product, bread.

Bread *containing* beans is another matter entirely, and predates the Boston combination by many centuries. In the Old Testament, for instance, the prophet Ezekiel (chapter 4, verse 9) at the Lord's bidding lived for three hundred and ninety days on a diet of water, meat, and bread made from wheat, barley, millet, beans, and lentils. An enterprising gentleman in the pulse-growing area of Ontario is actually marketing what he calls "Ezekiel flour."

This chapter contains close-to-home recipes such as dill-flavored, cheese and parsley topped bread, as well as some far-away ideas from Egypt, Lebanon, and West Africa.

Dilly Bean Bread

When nothing else will grow, due to strange weather or insects or the deer who love anything green around my place, I can still count on dill. I dry it, freeze it, grow it indoors all year round, and use it in as many recipes as I can. Witness this recipe for bean bread flavored with dill – a crusty, delicious taste treat!

2	tbsp	butter	30	mL
2	tbsp	finely chopped onion	30	mL
1	cup	bean puree	250	mL
1	tsp	salt	5	mL
2	tsp	dried dill weed	10	mL
1	tbsp	active dry yeast	15	mL
1	cup	lukewarm water	250	mL
2	tbsp	sugar	30	mL
3½–4	cups	flour	875	mL–1 L
1		egg	1	
½	tbsp	coarse salt	7	mL
2	tbsp	grated Parmesan cheese	30	mL
1	tbsp	chopped fresh parsley	15	mL

Notes: If you have fresh dill, use ¼ – ½ cup (50 – 125 mL) chopped fresh dill weed in this recipe. Prepare bean puree according to instructions on page 8. Great Northern, pink, or pinto beans would work well.

Melt butter in a small frying pan and sauté onion until tender but not browned. Add bean puree, salt, and dill weed. Mix well, remove from heat, and allow to cool until lukewarm.

In a large bowl, dissolve yeast in lukewarm water and sugar. Add lukewarm bean mixture and mix well. Stir in enough flour to make a stiff dough. Turn out onto a floured board and knead until smooth and elastic. Butter inside of the bowl, return dough to the bowl, and coat top of dough with a bit more soft butter. Cover lightly and put in a warm, draft-free spot until double in size.

Grease a bundt pan, a large bread pan, or two smaller bread pans. Punch down dough and shape to fit whatever pan or pans you are using. Put into pan and with a very sharp knife, slash several times about ¼ inch (1 cm) deep in top of loaf. Brush top with lightly beaten egg. Mix salt, Parmesan cheese, and parsley and sprinkle over loaf. Cover and let rise again until double in size, about 30 to 45 minutes. Bake in a 375°F (190°C) oven for 30 to 40 minutes or until loaf is golden brown and sounds hollow when tapped. Remove from pan and cool on a rack. Makes 1 large loaf or 2 small loaves.

The Cedars' Falafel

When my friend Mary Salloum opened The Cedars, a small restaurant and deli, I was pleased to be able to taste authentic Lebanese dishes using dried pulses. In Lebanon, falafel are tucked into pita bread and sold as commonly as hot dogs are sold in Canada!

1	lb	dried garbanzo beans	500	g
1		medium onion	1	
1		medium potato	1	
4		cloves garlic	4	
1	tsp	ground coriander	5	mL
1	tsp	cumin	5	mL
2	tsp	salt	10	mL
½	tsp	pepper	2	mL
½	tsp	cayenne	2	mL
1	tbsp	flour	15	mL
		Vegetable oil for frying the falafel		
2	tsp	baking soda	10	mL
		Sesame Seed Sauce (recipe follows)		

Soak garbanzos for 24 hours or at least overnight. Drain. Peel and quarter onion and potato. Run beans, onion, potato, and garlic through fine holes of a food grinder or put everything in a food processor and blend to a smooth paste. Remove to a bowl and add spices, seasonings, and flour. Mix well. If using a food grinder, run through the grinder again. Cover and let rest for 2 to 3 hours.

Heat oil for deep-fat frying. While oil is heating, add baking soda to the bean mixture. With dampened hands, form mixture into balls the size of a walnut, then flatten slightly into a pattie. Deep fry, making sure patties are cooked through and golden brown. Remove from oil with slotted spoon and drain on paper towels.

Serve as a meatless luncheon dish by tucking the falafel into a pita pocket and adding sliced radishes, chopped parsley, diced tomatoes, pickles, and hot peppers. Then add Sesame Seed Sauce. Falafel are also nice served as an appetizer with a bowl of hummus on the side. (You will find a recipe for hummus on page 16.) Makes about 50 walnut-sized falafel.

Sesame Seed Sauce

This is good with the falafel described above, but it's also nice served as a dip for breads and raw vegetables or as a dressing for any raw or cooked vegetable salad. Tahini, the sesame seed paste, is available in specialty stores or you can make your own.

1		clove garlic	1	
½	tsp	salt	2	mL
½	cup	Tahini (see page 17)	125	mL
½	cup	cold water	125	mL
½	cup	fresh lemon juice	125	mL

Crush garlic and salt together in a mixing bowl. Blend in Tahini. Gradually add water, blending well. Then blend in the lemon juice until smooth. If a thicker sauce is preferred, use less water. You could also make this with a blender or food processor, quick as a wink. Makes about 1½ cups (375 mL).

Tamia, Bean Pancakes

In Canada, we make potato pancakes. In Egypt, the equivalent is tamia, a delicious blend of beans and eggs.

1	lb	dried pea beans	500	g
2	tsp	salt	10	mL
2	tbsp	minced onion	25	mL
¼	cup	minced fresh parsley	50	mL
2		cloves garlic, crushed	2	
2	tbsp	flour	30	mL
2		eggs, beaten	2	
2	tbsp	butter or margarine	25	mL
2	tbsp	vegetable oil	25	mL

Prepare dried beans according to instructions on pages 5 and 6. Cover drained beans with fresh water, add salt, bring to a boil for 10 minutes, and then simmer for 45 minutes to 1 hour until beans are tender but not mushy. Drain again and save the water this time.

Mix beans with onion, parsley, and garlic. Puree through a food mill or in a blender, adding just enough of the reserved water to prevent sticking. To the pureed mixture, add flour and eggs. Mix well.

In a large heavy frying pan, heat butter with oil. The oil should be about 1 inch (2 cm) deep, and it should be very hot. Drop heaping tablespoonfuls of the bean mixture into the hot oil, flatten into pancake shapes, and fry on both sides until crusty and golden. Drain on paper towels and keep hot in a preheated 300°F (150°C) oven until ready to serve. Makes about 36.

Akara, Bean Fritters

These West African bean fritters remind me somewhat of Hush Puppies – the fried corn cakes, that is, not the shoes. Sometimes recipes calling for black-eyed peas leave out the presoaking, but in this case it must be done because of the short cooking time. So be prepared!

1	cup	dried black-eyed peas	250	mL
⅓	cup	chopped onion	75	mL
¼	cup	chopped fresh parsley	50	mL
1		egg	1	
2	tsp	minced fresh ginger root	10	mL
½	tsp	minced garlic	2	mL
1	tsp	whole cumin seeds	5	mL
1	tsp	ground coriander	5	mL
1	tsp	salt	5	mL
¼	tsp	cayenne pepper	1	mL
		Vegetable oil for deep-fat frying		
		Parsley Sauce (recipe follows)		

Note: The basic akara batter can be varied by adding finely minced vegetables. Okra is a popular addition in West Africa.

Prepare the black-eyed peas by one of the methods outlined on pages 5 and 6. Drain. In a food processor or blender, in several batches if necessary, mix peas and all the remaining ingredients for the fritters, making a coarse puree.

Heat oil in a deep-fat fryer or heavy saucepan until it reaches 375°F (190°C). Drop tablespoonfuls of fritter batter into the hot fat, about 4 or 5 at a time, cooking until crisp and brown, about 2 minutes. Remove with slotted spoon, drain on paper towels, and keep warm until all fritters are fried.

Serve the fritters hot, passing Parsley Sauce for dipping. Makes 8 to 10 appetizer-sized fritters or 4 large ones.

Akara has many forms. The batter can also be formed around whole, shelled, hard-cooked eggs, which are then lowered into hot, deep fat (375°F/190°C) and fried gently until brown. To serve, cut each egg in half and top with Parsley Sauce. Akara meatballs can also be made by combining the batter with ground beef, forming into balls, and frying in either deep fat or in ½ inch (1 cm) fat in a frying pan.

Parsley Sauce

½	cup	chopped fresh parsley	125	mL
¼	cup	oil	50	mL
3	tbsp	fresh lemon juice	50	mL

¼	tbsp	grated lemon rind	1	mL
¼	tsp	ground coriander	1	mL
¼	tsp	ground cumin	1	mL
¼	tsp	salt	1	mL

Combine all the ingredients in a blender and puree until nearly smooth. Makes about 1 cup (250 mL).

Desserts

Beans sometimes have an "image" problem. They are seen as sensible and nutritious and all that, but they're not perceived as sexy, exciting, or trendy. It's too bad because beans can be all those things . . . and more!

I hope this book will convince you to take a new look at beans and to try them in ways you've never considered before. For instance, have you considered using beans in desserts? They add moistness in much the same way as grated carrot or zucchini does, and they bring along all those other good things such as protein, vitamin B, and iron. Adding beans to your recipes is one way to rid yourself of the guilt we often feel about "empty calories" in desserts. You'll be creating a tasty and nutritious product. It's the best way to have your cake and eat it too!

Great Northern Torte

Although this sounds like the title of a book on railways, it's actually a recipe for a very tasty, rather unusual dessert – a torte made of the white beans called Great Northern. This variety of bean is my favorite and once you talk your local store into stocking it, my guess is you'll never go back to the navy or pea beans again. Great Northerns cook to the tender stage needed for puree in this recipe much faster than the other white beans do.

¾	cup	dried Great Northern beans	175	mL
3		eggs, separated	3	
¾	cup	Vanilla Sugar (recipe follows)	175	mL
2	tbsp	rum	25	mL
1¼	cups	ground nuts	300	mL
½	cup	apricot jam	125	mL
		Icing sugar		

Notes: If you don't have vanilla sugar made ahead of time you can use regular sugar plus ½ tsp (2 mL) vanilla extract. As for the nuts, you may use walnuts, hazelnuts, or pecans.

Soak beans by either of the methods outlined on pages 5 and 6. Cover with fresh water and cook over medium heat for about an hour, or until beans are tender. Drain and allow to dry off in a colander. Push beans through a food mill in order to get a very fine bean puree. You could use a blender or food processor but your final product won't be quite as fine.

Beat egg yolks with half the sugar until light. Gradually add the bean puree and rum. Mix well until batter is creamy and light. Fold in ground nuts.

Beat egg whites until soft peaks form. Gradually add remaining sugar, beating until whites become very stiff. Fold whites into the bean batter. Pour into well-greased and floured 9 inch (23 cm) spring-form pan. Bake in a 350°F (180°C) oven for about an hour or until the torte is firm and shrinks from the side of the pan. Let stand overnight.

The next day, carefully remove torte from pan, split into two layers, and spread apricot jam between the layers. Dust top with icing sugar.

Vanilla Sugar

To make vanilla sugar, keep a jar with a secure screw top filled with granulated sugar. Poke a vanilla bean down into the sugar and the flavor will permeate the sugar in about a week. Refill the jar as needed – the bean can be used for months. Vanilla beans are sold in most supermarkets.

Mock Pecan Pie

Here is an idea for making a pie using pureed beans. The recipe was passed on to me by a friend, Marg Bullis, whose family still thinks it's the real thing! The beans must be well cooked and not seasoned before pureeing.

		Pastry for single-crust 9 inch (23 cm) deep-dish pie		
½	cup	butter or margarine	125	mL
2	cups	sugar	500	mL
4		eggs, well beaten	4	
2	tbsp	golden corn syrup	25	mL
½	tsp	salt	2	mL
1	cup	unseasoned pureed pinto beans	250	mL
2	tsp	vanilla	10	mL
		Pecans for garnish		

Note: Prepare bean puree according to instructions on page 8.

Line pie plate with pie crust. Cream butter with sugar. Add eggs, syrup, and salt; beat well. Blend in bean puree and vanilla. Pour into lined pie shell. Cover with pecans or simply (in the interests of economy) scatter pecans over top of pie. Bake at 350°F (180°C) for about 45 minutes or until firm. Makes one 9 inch (23 cm) deep-dish pie.

Mexican Bean Cake

Mexican meals don't usually include cake, but this one – made with bean puree and lots of fruit and spices – would fit right in with Mexican food!

⅓	cup	butter or margarine	75	mL
¾	cup	sugar	175	mL
1		egg	1	
2	cups	unseasoned pinto bean puree	500	mL
2	tsp	vanilla extract	10	mL
1	cup	flour	250	mL
1	tsp	baking soda	5	mL
½	tsp	salt	2	mL
1	tsp	ground cinnamon	5	mL
½	tsp	ground cloves	2	mL
½	tsp	ground allspice	2	mL
2	cups	peeled and diced apple	500	mL
1	cup	raisins	250	mL
½	cup	chopped nuts	125	mL
1½	cups	icing sugar	375	mL
		Milk or fruit juice		

Preheat oven to 350°F (180°C). Grease and flour the bottom only of a 9 by 13 inch (22 by 33 cm) rectangular pan.

Cream butter with sugar. Add egg and beat well. Blend in bean puree and vanilla. In a separate bowl, combine flour, baking soda, salt, and spices. Mix with the apple, raisins, and nuts. Add dry ingredients and fruit to creamed mixture and blend well. Pour batter into prepared pan and bake 30 to 45 minutes or until cake tests done when tried with a toothpick.

Mix icing sugar with enough milk or fruit juice to make a thin glaze; drizzle over the still-warm cake. Keep in the refrigerator.

Harvest Moon Pie

If the frost got your garden pumpkins before you did, or if the cupboard is bare of pumpkin just when you're dying for a taste of pumpkin pie, do not despair. Use bean puree!

		Pastry for single-crust 9 inch (23 cm) deep-dish pie		
3		eggs	3	
2	cups	unseasoned bean puree	500	mL
1		can (14 oz/385 mL) evaporated milk	1	
1	cup	sugar	250	mL
½	tsp	salt	2	mL
½–1	tsp	cinnamon	2–5	mL
½–1	tsp	ground ginger	2–5	mL
¼	tsp	ground cloves	1	mL
¼	tsp	ground nutmeg	1	mL
		Whipped cream		

Note: You'll get the best-looking "pumpkin" pie with a puree made of pinto beans, but other beans will do if you cover it all up with whipped cream! Prepare bean puree according to instructions on page 8. Line pie plate with pie crust. Preheat oven to 375°F (190°C).

In a large bowl, beat eggs well. Add bean puree and milk, and stir until smooth. A large wire whip does a good job here. Add sugar, salt, and spices. Stir until blended. Pour into unbaked pie shell. Bake 1 hour or until knife blade inserted in center comes out clean. Cool at room temperature and then refrigerate. Serve chilled with whipped cream. Makes one 9 inch (23 cm) deep-dish pie.

Red Bean Desserts, Guri Guri and Popsicles!

In China and Japan particularly, a small, round deep-red bean is so popular it is called the "King of the Beans." We can often find it in our local stores under the name of adzuki, azuki, or aduki. Because it has a light nutty flavor, it's the one most often used in bean desserts. And if you've been to Hawaii lately, you'll know about Guri Guri, a dessert that combines scoops of sherbet with a sweet red-bean sauce – something like our ice cream sundaes.

10	oz	dried adzuki beans	300	g
2		slices fresh ginger root	2	
1	tbsp	grated orange rind	15	mL
		Water to cover beans generously		
½	cup	white sugar	125	mL
1½	cups	brown sugar	375	mL

Wash red beans three to four times until water comes nice and clear. In a 4 quart (4 L) heavy saucepan, combine beans, ginger root, and orange rind. Cover with at least three times as much water as beans, bring to a boil for 10 minutes, cover, and simmer 1½ to 2 hours or until beans are tender. Drain beans, add sugars, and simmer another 10 minutes until sugars are dissolved. Serve hot as a pudding with cream or milk, or cold over scoops of sherbet, or freeze the mixture and serve like a popsicle. Makes 4 cups (1 L) red bean sauce.

Portuguese Bean Custard Tarts

These tarts have a melted sugar glaze and powdery top hats. If you don't have straight-sided tart tins, you can use muffin tins instead. For easy removal after baking, butter the tins and then line them with your best lard-based pastry.

2½	cups	sugar	625	mL
1	cup	water	250	mL
¼	cup	unseasoned white bean puree	50	mL
½	cup	flour	125	mL
3		large eggs	3	
		Icing sugar		

Note: You can make the bean puree from canned or home-cooked white kidney beans, white lima beans, Great Northern, or navy beans. See instructions on page 8.

In a heavy-bottomed saucepan, make a syrup of sugar and water, stirring until sugar is dissolved. Then, without stirring, bring to a boil and boil gently 20 to 25 minutes until the soft ball stage is reached (227°F/115°C on a candy thermometer). Remove from stove and let cool slightly.

Meanwhile, mix bean puree and flour. In another bowl, beat eggs well. When the syrup is cool but before it begins to harden, pour it into the flour/bean mixture, beating at high speed until you have a smooth thick syrup. Beat in eggs and then strain through a sieve.

Carefully ladle the filling into the pastry-lined tins to within ⅛ inch (0.5 cm) of the top. Fill in the space left with a generous layer of icing sugar. Wipe any spills or sugar from the pan. Bake in a 400°F (200°C) oven for 35 minutes or until the filling rises and the sugar has melted into a golden brown crust with a dusting of unmelted sugar on top. Let stand in tins for 2 to 3 minutes, then remove carefully and allow to cool on a rack. Store in an airtight container.

This filling is enough for twenty 2 inch (5 cm) tarts.

Fresh Apple-Bean Cake with Fruit Topping

This nutritious cake recipe, reprinted with the kind permission of the Pulse Growers Association of Alberta, is best when allowed to age for a day or two. It's a moist and tasty addition to lunch boxes.

2	cups	cooked beans	500	mL
¼	cup	bean liquid or apple juice	75	mL
¾	cup	vegetable oil	175	mL
¾	cup	sugar	175	mL
¾	cup	brown sugar	175	mL
2		eggs	2	
1	tsp	vanilla	5	mL
1½	cups	whole wheat flour	375	mL
2	tsp	baking powder	10	mL
½	tsp	salt	2	mL
1	tsp	cinnamon	5	mL
½	tsp	ground cloves	2	mL
2	cups	unpeeled, finely chopped apples	500	mL
		Fruit Topping (recipe follows)		

Note: Great Northern, pinto, or pink beans could be used.

Place cooked beans and bean liquid or apple juice into a blender or food processor and puree until smooth. In a large mixing bowl, beat oil with sugars until dissolved. Add eggs and continue beating. Add bean puree and vanilla. Mix well. Combine dry ingredients and add to bean mixture. Blend well. Stir in apple. Pour into greased 8 by 12 inch (3 L) baking pan and bake at 350°F (180°C) for 35 to 45 minutes. Cool and frost with Fruit Topping.

Fruit Topping

⅔	cup	sugar	150	mL
3		egg yolks	3	
½	cup	butter or margarine	125	mL
½	cup	raisins	125	mL
½	cup	coconut	125	mL
½	cup	chopped walnuts	125	mL

In a small heavy saucepan or double boiler, mix sugar with egg yolks. Add butter and raisins. Cook until thick. Stir in coconut and nuts. Spread topping on cooled Apple-Bean Cake.

Bean and Apple Crumble

Here's a new and different version of the traditional Apple Betty, equally as delicious as the original but a bit more nutritious with the addition of beans.

½	cup	dried adzuki beans	125	mL
1	lb	cooking apples	500	g
½–1	tsp	cinnamon	2–5	mL
		Honey to taste		
		Water, if necessary		
¾	cup	quick rolled oats	200	mL
½	cup	oat-flake cereal	125	mL
¼	cup	whole wheat flour	50	mL
½	cup	shredded coconut	125	mL
3	tbsp	salad oil	50	mL

Note: You could use 2 cups (500 mL) applesauce in place of the cooking apples.

Soak beans by either method outlined on pages 5 and 6. To the drained beans, add double the amount of water and simmer, covered, until beans are tender. Drain well and mash.

Peel apples, cut in quarters, and cook in a small amount of water until soft. Mix with the mashed beans. Season apple/bean mixture with cinnamon and sweeten with as much honey as needed. Add water if the mixture is too dry. It should be the consistency of thick applesauce. Grease an 8 by 8 inch (20 by 20 cm) pan or large casserole dish. Place the apple/bean mixture into bottom of the pan.

Mix rolled oats, cereal, flour, coconut, and salad oil together. Spread evenly on a greased cookie sheet or baking sheet. Place in a 350°F (180°C) oven for 3 to 4 minutes, just until the crumble is a light brown. Stir occasionally and keep a sharp eye on it so that it doesn't get overdone.

Remove from oven, sprinkle over the apple/bean mixture, and bake at 350°F (180°C) 20 to 25 minutes, until the top is golden brown and crisp. If the crisp is getting too brown, cover lightly with foil, baking just long enough to heat apple layer through.

This crumble is delicious served hot or cold with pouring cream, whipped cream, or ice cream. Makes 5 or 6 generous servings.

Maple Syrup Pie

Yes, maple syrup pie made with beans! But don't tell your guests until they taste it. They'll never believe it, but they will line up for more pie. It's delicious!

		Pastry for single-crust 9 inch (23 cm) deep-dish pie		
1½	cups	maple syrup	375	mL
3	tbsp	cornstarch	50	mL
2	tbsp	water	30	mL
3		eggs, separated	3	
½	cup	butter	125	mL
1	cup	unseasoned bean puree	250	mL
⅛	tsp	cream of tartar	0.5	mL
⅓	cup	brown sugar	75	mL
1	tsp	vanilla	5	mL

Line pie plate with pie crust. Boil maple syrup for 5 minutes. In a small bowl, mix cornstarch with water, stirring until all lumps are worked out. Add to the hot syrup and cook, stirring constantly, until mixture is smooth and transparent, about 2 to 3 minutes.

In another small bowl, beat egg yolks, add a bit of the hot syrup, beating well, and then put it all back into the hot maple syrup. This warms up the eggs so that they don't curdle or cook until completely mixed in. Add butter and bean puree and allow to cool.

Pour into unbaked crust and bake in a 350°F (180°C) oven for 40 to 50 minutes or until knife inserted in center comes out clean. Allow to cool slightly while making the meringue.

In a glass or metal bowl (not plastic), beat egg whites until frothy. Add cream of tartar and continue beating at a high speed. Gradually add brown sugar and vanilla. Continue beating until meringue will hold up in peaks when the beaters are lifted. Spread on pie, making sure it is sealed to the outer edge. Bake 10 to 15 minutes until lightly browned.

Serve at room temperature. It's not likely, but if you have any left over, keep it in the refrigerator until it is eaten. Makes one 9 inch (23 cm) deep-dish pie.

Yaki Manju, Japanese Tea Cakes

You never know where you're going to find a bean recipe. This one came to me via Norma Bannerman, who went to the hairdresser's one day and tasted one of her hairdresser's homemade bean cakes. It was delicious, and Rita Nishikawa gave us her recipe.

Anko Bean Filling

1½	cups	dried small red beans	375	mL
3	cups	sugar	750	mL

Cake Mixture

½	cup	butter or margarine	125	mL
¾	cup	sugar	175	mL
1		egg	1	
2	cups	flour	500	mL
1	tsp	baking powder	5	mL
½	tsp	baking soda	2	mL
		Dash of salt		
⅓	cup	milk	75	mL

Glaze

1		egg yolk	1	
2	tsp	milk	10	mL
		Sesame seeds (optional)		

To make the filling, soak beans according to one of the methods outlined on pages 5 and 6. Cover drained beans with double the amount of cold water. Bring to a boil and boil for 2 minutes. Drain again. Cover again with double the amount of fresh water. Heat to simmering point and simmer, covered, until very tender, about 1½ hours. Drain.

Mash beans with a potato masher until mixture is quite fine. Place into a heavy saucepan. Add sugar and heat over low heat until sugar is dissolved. Mixture becomes quite liquid at this point. Cook over low to medium heat for about 40 minutes until mixture becomes thick again. Stir frequently to prevent scorching. Use in tea cakes as outlined below. Store any unused filling in refrigerator.

To make the tea cake mixture, cream butter and sugar until light; add egg and beat well. Combine dry ingredients and add alternately with milk to the creamed mixture. Dough should be soft but still hold its shape when baked. To test, shape one small piece of dough into a round ball and bake in a 375°F (190°C) oven for 12 to 14 minutes. If the cookie flattens too much, add a little more flour. If it's too stiff, add a little more milk.

118

Divide dough into 36 portions about 1 tbsp (15 mL) each. Shape into round balls. Flatten and place about 1 tsp (5 mL) of bean filling in center. Wrap dough around filling and press edges together. Place tea cakes on a greased baking sheet. Mix egg yolk and milk and brush over tea cakes to glaze. Sprinkle with sesame seeds, if desired. Bake at 375°F (190°C) for 12 to 14 minutes or until lightly browned. Makes about 3 dozen.

Index

About the author

Jean Hoare has been interested in cooking and serving special meals from an early age. In Toronto, where she grew up, she and a ten-year old friend would prepare an elaborate dinner for their families every Friday night. After graduating from high school during the Great Depression and finding a job in the buying office of the Hudson's Bay Company, Jean was soon sampling the delights of as many downtown Toronto restaurants as her meagre salary would allow.

During the war she married and in 1946 she and her husband settled in southern Alberta. In 1956 she realized her childhood dream and opened her own restaurant, the Driftwood Room, right in her ranch home. Its reputation grew and in 1966 she moved the restaurant into an old NATO supply depot nearby and renamed it The Flying N. From 1972 to 1974 The Flying N was twice named one of the best ten restaurants in Canada. In 1975, after nearly twenty years in the restaurant business, she decided to sell.

Since retiring from the restaurant business, Jean has devoted her time to pursuing her interest in food and cooking. She wrote the best-selling *Best Little Cookbook in the West* and starred in the television cooking show "Town and Country Cooking." She has traveled across the country giving cooking demonstrations and lessons.

Jean is a member of the International Wine and Food society and her goal is to "eat her way around the world." Her international travels with this organization have given her the opportunity to collect an extensive list of exotic and unusual recipes, many of which appear in this book. When not traveling, Jean's leisure activities center around country life in the foothills of Alberta.